GAME CHANGER

Game **CHANGER**

The Remarkable Story of Caroline's Cart

Drew Ann Long
with Bethany Bradsher

Whitecaps Media
Houston

Whitecaps Media
Houston, Texas
whitecapsmedia.com

Game Changer: The Remarkable Story of Caroline's Cart

Hardback ISBN: 978-1-942732-15-0
Paperback ISBN: 978-1-942732-16-7
eBook ISBN: 978-1-942732-18-1

Printed in the United States of America

Drew Long and Bethany Bradsher may be reached through the publisher (wcm@whitecapsmedia.com)

To all my fellow dreamers out there,
those who have succeeded
and all of you who are still striving—
this is for you

It is not the critic who counts;
not the man who points out how the
strong man stumbles, or where the doer
of deeds could have done them better.
The credit belongs to the man who is
actually in the arena, whose face is
marred by dust and sweat and blood;
who strives valiantly; who errs, who
comes short again and again, because
there is no effort without error and
shortcoming; but who does actually
strive to do the deeds; who knows great
enthusiasms, the great devotions; who
spends himself in a worthy cause; who
at the best knows in the end the triumph
of high achievement, and who at the
worst, if he fails, at least fails while
daring greatly, so that his place shall
never be with those cold and timid souls
who neither know victory nor defeat.

Theodore Roosevelt

Contents

Never give in, never give in, never, never, never, never—in nothing, great or small, large or petty—never give in except to convictions of honour and good sense.

Winston Churchill

Introduction

A Trip to the Grocery Store

"WHAT DO YOU MEAN WE DON'T HAVE ANY SNACKS?" I asked in disbelief. "And the sweet tea is gone, too?"

It was a hot summer day in 2007. I had three children ages ten and under and the pantry was nearly bare. If you've ever been to Alabama in July, you know that *emergency* is not a strong enough word for that situation.

"Okay, get your shoes on. We're heading to the grocery store."

Like it or not, I had to work up the energy to make a grocery run with all three kids. A shopping trip with three children requires courage and fortitude under the best of circumstances, but my situation was considerably more complicated than that of the typical mom.

My daughter Caroline has Rett Syndrome, a neurological disorder that has rendered her unable to walk or talk. When our oldest daughter Mary Grace was ten, Caroline was six, and my son Matthew had just turned three, and any trip to our local grocery store—even for just a loaf of bread and a dozen eggs—involved a dizzying series of steps and considerations.

That July day I packed up Caroline's diaper bag and other necessities (including her Shrek doll—she never goes anywhere without it) and put those items in the car along with her forty-pound wheelchair, which took up half of the trunk space in my minivan. I checked that everyone had shoes on and had been to the bathroom, carried Caroline out to the car to buckle her into her car seat, and made sure Matthew and Mary Grace were secure in their seats as well.

Once we arrived at the store, I parked in the handicapped space, which thankfully was available (not always the case!), and made sure the kids knew their assignments.

Mary Grace asked, "Can I push the shopping cart?"

"No, it's better if you push Caroline in the wheelchair because Matthew will be in the cart and it's harder to steer."

I unloaded the wheelchair, settled Caroline into her seat, and then, once inside the store, buckled Matthew into the front of the cart. Soon our little caravan—wheelchair and shopping cart—was weaving up and down the aisles under my direction. Suffice it to say we never flew under the radar at the grocery store.

That arrangement, with Mary Grace pushing one vehicle and me controlling the other, was actually the best-case scenario. If grocery shopping was necessary when Mary Grace was in school or at dance class and my husband David was on a business trip, I would have to employ what special-needs families refer to as "the train," in which I pushed the shopping cart and Matthew with one hand and pulled the wheelchair with the other down the serpentine grocery aisles, all while trying to check off every item on my list and therefore ensure that my next grocery trip would be as far in the future as possible. Once in a while, daunted by the prospect of such a labor-intensive outing, I would hire a babysitter just so that I could do the shopping.

Sometimes when both Mary Grace and Matthew were elsewhere or I felt Matthew could walk along with me, I would take only the wheelchair into the store, but that method meant that I could only buy the items I could pile on top of Caroline's lap. A couple of times I even arranged a blanket in the basket of the cart and laid Caroline on top of it—until a store manager stopped me and told me I couldn't put her in the cart basket anymore. The cart wasn't designed for that purpose, he informed me, and the store could not insure her safety if she rode that way.

Of course, when I had finally selected my groceries (making sure I remembered at least a gallon of my favorite Milo's sweet tea) and made our way through the checkout line, I had to be on hyper alert to safely steer the train through the precariously busy parking lot, pick Caroline up out of her wheelchair and settle her into her car seat, make sure the other two kids were secure, fold up the wheelchair, replace it in the back of the van, load the groceries (praying they would fit in the space next to the wheelchair in the back), return the grocery cart, and drive home, only to face the task of unloading the children and all of the groceries when we pulled into the garage. I felt a pretty huge sense of accomplishment that I had pulled off another shopping trip and, in the way one prays for a miracle, hoped that somehow this food supply wouldn't become depleted so I wouldn't have to return to the grocery store anytime soon.

There was a time, until Caroline reached the age of four or five, when she would fit into one of the toddler carts, or "amusement carts," that many grocery stores provide for preschoolers. If I was lucky, I could secure a double amusement cart for Caroline and Matthew and Mary Grace could walk alongside. Now, that was a victory. But once Caroline outgrew that particular cart style, the real grocery store headaches for my family began.

More than once in those years, when I was piloting my little caravan through the store like the grand marshal at a parade, I would pass an adult driving a grocery scooter—you've seen them, those self-propelled vehicles with a basket attached for those who lack the mobility to walk through the store. The more I saw the scooters, the amusement carts, and the carts designed for mothers with babies, the more one question burned in my heart: *How*, I wondered, *could a store provide for those with limited mobility because of age or other health conditions and go to great lengths to keep babies, toddlers, and preschoolers placated while their parents shopped, yet do nothing to serve older children and adults with special needs?* Why was there no accommodation that would allow a child like Caroline to participate in a shopping trip with her family?

That was the question that birthed a calling in me and launched what seemed like a simple mission—to create and distribute a shopping cart for special-needs children. If I needed a cart designed for Caroline this desperately, I reasoned, plenty of other moms and dads in other places needed it too. As my "simple" quest became unthinkably complicated and expensive, and one dead end after another threatened my resolve, I persevered because I believed I was on a journey ordained by God and, ultimately, if He meant for the cart to succeed it would succeed.

As I have told everyone from engineers to store managers and lawyers, I am just a mom from Alabaster, Alabama, with a simple wish: that my family and others like it can go shopping in a more simple and dignified way. The nearly decade-long odyssey that made Caroline's Cart a reality—and the pitfalls and victories that God allowed along the way—are ultimately a testament to His great faithfulness.

But an unexpected way
On this unexpected day
Could it mean this is where I belong
It is you I have loved all along

Shrek

1

Caroline

WHEN WE BROUGHT OUR SECOND daughter Caroline home from the hospital in October 2000, the only thing we had to worry about was making the transition from one child to two. Caroline was a beautiful, healthy baby, with higher scores on the newborn APGAR test than our firstborn daughter Mary Grace. She was a strong nurser, held her head up on her own earlier than Mary Grace had and, in the first several months, achieved each developmental milestone on schedule or earlier.

I had earned a business degree from Louisiana State University and moved to the Birmingham area—a city where I knew no one—a few years after graduation to take a job at an engineering firm. I soon met David, who went to high school with my college roommate, and in 1995—two years after I had settled in Alabama—we were married. At the time of Caroline's birth we hadn't quite reached a compromise for the size of our family (I wanted a big family; David wasn't so sure). But we agreed that we would have at least two, and when Caroline arrived early in the new millennium we were thrilled.

Soon we fell into the rhythms of juggling two children with distinct needs and schedules and life was good with our little family. I went back to work (by that time I had taken a position as the financial director of a boarding school). David was traveling a good bit for his job with a student loan company and we had no extended family nearby, so the adjustment was certainly chaotic at times. I was just starting to establish confidence in our new routine when I was forced, when Caroline was nine months old, to face the reality that she might not be as typical and healthy as we had hoped.

It would be several years before we had an official name for the deterioration we were starting to notice, but in retrospect we were witnessing the cruel reversal that strikes every Rett Syndrome family.

Caused by a genetic mutation, Rett strikes mostly girls, and it is found in about one in every ten thousand female births. We spotted red flags before Caroline's first birthday, but in most Rett cases development continues on a fairly normal schedule until eighteen or twenty-four months, and then the child begins to regress visibly. Experts call this phase of the disorder "rapid destruction," and in most Rett girls it starts between the ages of one and four and continues until they enter the next stage, known as "plateau."

David remembers those losses—the things we once saw Caroline do that slowly disappeared—as a particularly cruel part of our journey toward her diagnosis and our acceptance.

"For the first year and a half you have a typical child, and you don't have a clue that anything is wrong, zero," David recalls. "You think you have a perfectly happy baby. So a little bit after a year old, that's when she started regressing. And that's when you start asking questions. And as parents there is this period of total denial. 'What do you mean we don't have a perfectly healthy child? That's what I had, that's what you sent home with me, that's what I've been raising for over a year.'

"And what's worse about that, they tell you that she's going to get worse. She's going to regress, and she'll also start having seizures soon. You see this dexterity with her hands? That's going to go. This cruising, holding onto the furniture? That's going to go. What was horrible for me, it seems if you gain this milestone, you don't lose that, right? If babies can cruise and babble and feed Cheerios to themselves, it was just unfathomable for me that they would lose it. And that's exactly what happened."

Caroline was close to her first birthday before I worked up the nerve to voice my concerns to my pediatrician, who reassured me, telling me she was just fine, only a little sicklier than most babies, and that I shouldn't compare her development to Mary Grace's. Caroline's delays became more pronounced and we asked questions of more doctors—something we had plenty of opportunity to do because Caroline was sick most of the time. In retrospect, her eventful medical history in the first eighteen months of life was one of the things that masked the Rett diagnosis, because her fragile immune system, as well as unusual characteristics like extreme obesity starting at about twelve months, were not typical Rett symptoms.

At some point in those early years, I typed up Caroline's medical history so that I could have it handy on doctor's visits. To see it all in black and white is mind-boggling. In her first year, Caroline had twelve fevers, five ear infections, and six antibiotic prescriptions. By the age of two she had suffered fifteen ear infections and received fifteen antibiotics, and by her fourth birthday she had already taken twenty-nine different schedules of antibiotics. She was also extremely obese, especially from twelve to twenty-four months, and even though fevers and ear infections struck her the most commonly, she also suffered from multiple rashes, at least three cases of strep throat, and four sinus infections—all by the time she turned four. It seemed like we lived at the pediatrician's office.

As we researched childhood illnesses and disorders and made countless trips to an endless array of physicians, I had to quit my job, because motherhood had become more than a full-time job. Instead of finances, I became well versed in the world of childhood illnesses and disorders.

With so many infections and fevers being treated by so many antibiotics, combined with the denial of her developmental regression, it's no wonder we were slow to pin her with an official diagnosis. Before we accepted our designation as a Rett Syndrome family, we chased a series of other medical theories—a quest that took us to California four times for consultations with a doctor who specialized in immune system disorders.

We began regular consultations with the Los Angeles doctor—from the time Caroline was two until about her fourth birthday—because of our concerns about her malfunctioning immune system. Through countless scans and tests, the doctor correctly diagnosed Caroline with a cellular immunodeficiency, but when we brought up Rett Syndrome he dismissed the possibility.

It might seem crazy that we were jumping on planes and jetting across the country, but we wanted so badly for nothing to be seriously wrong with Caroline that we would have done anything to chase a hopeful word. In retrospect, if I were advising a mother facing a difficult diagnosis now, I would say, "Don't be afraid. Face it head on, decide who you're going to be through the trials, and trust God to give you strength." But in those years, I needed to keep pursuing possibilities as long as there was any glimmer of hope.

Through years of despair, false hopes, confusion, fear, and frequent trips to investigate the latest plausible theory, the Lord was preparing me to accept the reality of Caroline's medical situation by giving me the truth in small, progressive doses. We might have searched for every other possibility for more than four years, but I first heard about Rett Syndrome when Caroline was two—and in retrospect I believe I knew even then that our daughter had the disorder.

I had left her in the church nursery one Sunday, and when I returned after the service a young medical student was holding her. This young lady, the daughter-in-law of one of our nursery volunteers who just happened to be visiting that day, had observed Caroline's deteriorating motor skills and muscle control, and even though she was still a student she had heard of a condition that seemed to fit our daughter.

With what I'm sure was a bit of trepidation, she gently asked me, "Have you ever heard of Rett Syndrome?"

I hadn't, but I did what any desperate parent would do: I went home and Googled it. I opened a website, read the description, and burst into tears. Even though Caroline exhibited some symptoms that were atypical of Rett, I knew in my heart that this diagnosis fit my daughter. With Rett in the back of our minds, we continued our quest for a more hopeful answer, prayed, cared for our girls, and tried to put one foot in front of the other.

Finally, when Caroline was four years old, a Birmingham doctor made it official: Even though she was still exhibiting some unusual symptoms that didn't fall in line with typical Rett cases, the blood test, which identified the mutation of a gene called MECP2, was definitive proof of the diagnosis. Rett strikes most girls in four stages—early onset, rapid destruction, plateau, and late motor deterioration. By the time we had a name for Caroline's condition, the period of regression, or rapid destruction, was almost over, and when she was five she started a plateau period—she has had very little change for close to ten years.

Rett Syndrome is a very cruel disease, because every single Rett family brings home a healthy baby and is forced to face their medical reality a little bit at a time. But even if the realization was traumatizing that Caroline was different from the baby we met at the hospital, I believe that God knew I needed the gradual unveiling of the truth. It was, in a sense, a display of His grace that I had time to absorb and process each new loss, time to prepare for the difficult truth as I traveled down multiple dead-end roads. Parents who receive a devastating diagnosis seem to be either slapped in the face by the news or eased into it; the Lord knew my personality and He knew I needed the second way. It may sound crazy, but I believe God was good to me through those three years, giving me hope when I needed it and showing me in big and small ways that He would take care of my family no matter what.

Rett Syndrome has no cure—only recommendations for therapy and support for the children and families facing the disorder.

In some ways our medical mystery wasn't completely resolved, because even Rett specialists agreed that Caroline's symptoms put her in a class by herself. But with the diagnosis, we moved into a new phase—learning about the condition and figuring out what it meant for our family. I slowly began to accept our situation and even to seek joy within it, but I still spent many days crying and questioning God. And even as I tried to move to a place of acceptance, I continued to pray for healing. I knew God had the power to heal Caroline, and for years I begged Him to do it. Eventually, though, my prayers turned to something like, "Lord, give me the strength and courage to face this new normal. Whatever lies ahead, I know I can't do it alone."

I cried until I couldn't cry anymore, and I remember getting frustrated with David because he refused to wallow in the sadness with me. I didn't know this at the time, but the divorce rate in families with special-needs children is sky high; this could have destroyed our marriage. I remember desperately wishing I could be happy, but the reality of our situation was like a weight around my neck. I would wake up sad and overwhelmed. Whenever I was out in public or with friends I battled feelings of jealousy for families with healthy, able-bodied toddlers. Eventually I learned that happiness is a choice, and if I'm honest I have to admit there were plenty of days when I chose the opposite.

Through my grief, I saw David display a resolve rooted in his own faith in God and his conviction, even soon after the diagnosis, that the Lord would use this situation for His glory if we faced it with joy and faith. As we talked through it together, we realized that how we respond to Caroline's condition was part of her testimony—that God could use our daughter, even though she can't walk or talk, if we were open to what He was doing through her life.

Here's David: "I always make it a point, when you see me out with Caroline, I'm smiling. I see so many special-needs families who are angry, bitter, 'look what life's dealt me,' a lot of folks looking for sympathy. That never occurred to me. In fact, I shun that."

As we practiced choosing a positive outlook and worked through the days when tears were inevitable anyway, we couldn't have known how steely our resolve would have to be on the road ahead—how desperately we would need the faith and perseverance we were forging when Caroline was small to propel us into an unlikely leap of faith involving a shopping cart and the entire retail food industry.

Hardship often prepares an ordinary person for an extraordinary destiny.

Christopher Markus

2

And Then There Were Five

WHILE WE WERE STILL NAVIGATING the fog of Caroline's health issues, before we came to know her as one of the seventy-five girls with Rett's in Alabama at that time, I began to think and pray about having another child. I had always envisioned a home with lots of kids, and even though our life would always be more complicated than that of a typical family I didn't see that as an obstacle to bringing another Long into the world. In some ways, I think I was embracing the hope that adding another child to our family would represent—or I was just plain crazy.

David wasn't so sure. In fact, I think he thought I had lost my mind the first time I brought it up. Because of the roller coaster we had been riding with Caroline, his first fear was that we would have another child with special needs, even though the occurrence of Rett Syndrome is entirely random and has no known genetic family connection. I countered that we didn't want Mary Grace to have sole responsibility for Caroline after we were gone, and I told him that, whether by the grace of God or mother's intuition, I had absolutely no fear of lightning striking twice. But even if it did, I knew that we could handle that as well.

I asked David to pray about it, and over time the Lord just changed his heart. When I brought it up a few months later, he agreed we should try. That was late 2003, when Caroline was about to turn three and Mary Grace was soon to be six. Before we knew it, in the midst of the cross-country trips to California and the near-constant worry about Caroline's health, I was pregnant with baby number three.

I remember being so excited about the pregnancy, but when we started telling our family and friends some of them reacted with visible shock. When you have a special-needs child, no one can believe that you would voluntarily add another little person to the mix, and we were met with concern and confusion when we shared our news. It wasn't exactly the most encouraging start to this new chapter in our adventure, but in time our inner circle got on board with this idea and slowly began to share our anticipation for the day in August 2004 when our new baby—a boy!—would make his appearance.

Throughout the pregnancy, I was diligent about my diet and about regular prenatal care, just as I had been when I was expecting the girls. But because we were still in the throes of seeking the truth about Caroline and because her situation was part of our medical profile, I was considered a high-risk patient, and I faced an onslaught of advice from doctors about screenings that might reveal any health issues in our unborn baby. We refused every test. I finally started telling doctors, "I don't care if this baby is a monkey with a tail; I'm having it. You can give me every test you have, but no matter what you discover I'm not doing anything about it." And even though our worry about Caroline was nearly constant, I had a peace through that pregnancy that could only have come straight from God, because it didn't make sense to anyone around me.

Little baby Matthew came three weeks before his due date, in July 2004—a perfectly healthy baby (of course, we had heard those words before). I delivered by Caesarean section, which meant I had to spend four days in the hospital to recover. David couldn't stay with me because he had to take care of Caroline at home, so my six-year-old daughter became my number one helper. Mary Grace slept beside me in that hospital room, and whenever Matthew woke up crying I had to wake her up and coach her as she carefully handed him to me.

It was too much responsibility for such a young girl, but she rose to the occasion, and I don't know how I could have made it through those first days without her. The reality of how much more I suddenly had on my plate was crushing. I had been so sure about expanding our family and so confident that everything would be okay, but I remember crying out to God in the hospital, telling Him, "Lord, please help me."

Even later, when we were in our home and David was out of town, Mary Grace would sleep in my bed so that she could help me if I needed anything in the middle of the night. In some ways, she had to grow up quickly, but today both she and Matthew are exceptionally compassionate and tenderhearted—traits that were certainly forged in those wilderness years when I often needed them to support me, instead of the other way around.

We were thrilled with our son, but his timing—and the circumstances of our life that summer—couldn't have been worse. For a number of months, we had been watching the construction of our new house progress down the street from our old one. I had warned the contractor that I was expecting a baby in August and I really didn't love the idea of homelessness with a newborn. He assured me that the house would be completed in plenty of time.

Not only was the construction delayed, but our old house had sold and Matthew decided to make an early appearance. Just perfect. All of those factors converged to create this sad picture: Our newly expanded family of five, with an almost-four-year-old who couldn't do anything for herself, living in the Holiday Inn Express in nearby Pelham. We literally brought Matthew home from the hospital to a hotel room. We drive past that Holiday Inn Express all the time, and he always says, "There's my first home!"

We can laugh about it now, but that hot summer was one of the darkest chapters of my life. I was in recovery from a C-section so I couldn't lift Caroline or even stand up straight, we lived in a Holiday Inn, and David was busy with work all of the time. One day shortly after Matthew was born, David was driving us back to the hotel, and he looked over at me in the passenger seat and I was just sobbing. We always say that David's job is to keep me on a steady plain when I get either too high or too low, but that day he truly didn't know what to do with me.

He turned to me and asked, "What's the matter with you?"

I'm not sure I responded with either clarity or kindness. Needless to say, he never asked me that question again.

Friends from our Sunday school class brought us dinner in the hotel every other night. I was sleeping very little and crying all the time, until my mom took one too many tearful phone calls from me. She hopped in her car and came up from Slidell, Louisiana, and rented a room near ours. Eventually Mary Grace moved into Grammy's room, and after two weeks in the Holiday Inn—with David facing the prospects of several business trips—we left with my mom to go stay with her in Louisiana. We stayed with my mom for three more weeks, and finally, when Matthew was nearly six weeks old, we moved into our new house.

Surrounded by boxes, I was still overwhelmed by the amount of care all of these small people required, but at least we were in our own home. It was around this time that we received Caroline's official Rett's diagnosis, so in a sense the new house marked the beginning of our new reality—a family of five with a special-needs daughter who might stay the same or deteriorate, but never improve. Caroline couldn't walk or talk, feed herself, or go to the bathroom, and as she entered her plateau period, taking care of her was akin to caring for a baby.

Most days simply didn't contain enough hours to meet everyone's needs, and I collapsed into bed more nights than not. But even though the daily duties seemed impossibly taxing at times, David and I made some decisions very early that guided our attitudes from that point on. First of all, we weren't looking for people to feel sorry for us, and we knew with clarity that Caroline, with every one of her struggles, was exactly the child God meant to give us. We journeyed through denial, then through self-pity, and then one day, we agreed that this is the child we have, we weren't going to love her any less, and we would play the hand that was dealt us.

Second, we felt we could do it without a lot of extra help. Eventually Caroline would receive Alabama Medicaid, and along with that came a few hours a week of in-home nursing help, but we never wanted our other children to think that Caroline was a burden or that we weren't able to care for her. In time, I found a balance and learned that it was okay to ask for help when I needed it, especially when I had the opportunity to spend quality time one-on-one with Matthew or Mary Grace. Sometimes I had to accept help for the sake of the others in my family.

Our final resolution was related to the other two, and in many ways it was the initial spark that would eventually lead down a winding road to creating a special-needs grocery cart. We were a family, a closed circle in which Caroline was just as important as everyone else. We liked to be on the go. Consequently, we would do as many things as possible as a family. We have a pontoon boat on a nearby lake and we love to spend the day on the water; we didn't hesitate to bring Caroline along on those trips. Whether it was an amusement park, a restaurant, the mall, or the grocery store, we didn't love the idea of hiring a babysitter or a caregiver for one of our children so that we could go spend time with the others, if we could at all avoid it.

Sometimes I refer to that period as my pregame warm-up, because so many of those trials gave me strength for what was ahead. There were so many instances, when I faced major setbacks in the progress of the cart or in Caroline's health, when I told myself, "If I survived that, I can survive this."

I believe some people who have an entrepreneurial idea or a crazy dream start off with lots of energy, but if they have lived a fairly easy and comfortable life, they quit and return to the circumstances they can control the first time they hit a roadblock. We never had that option with Caroline's illness, and it made me stubbornly perseverant through the next challenge, a quality I would need like no other.

The takeaway from my story, and the word I hope will hit home with any parent who receives a devastating diagnosis, is this: I get the heartache. I get that you don't like what life has dealt you. I didn't either. But you are given a choice out of every situation life gives you. If I had been angry about Caroline I never would have had Matthew, because I would have been scared.

Not only that, I would never have had the optimism or the strength to endure the undertaking of bringing Caroline's Cart to life. David believes strongly that if we had been bitter and reluctant to accept Caroline's condition, God would have given the dream of the cart to someone else. It was in surrender that we were given an opportunity that would both stretch us and reward us beyond anything we could have imagined.

Only one who attempts the absurd is capable of achieving the impossible.

Miguel de Unamuno

3

Not So Easy-Peasy

THE PERIOD OF TIME AFTER Matthew's birth was certainly like an extended walk through the wilderness, but eventually the children grew older and more capable. I adjusted to the new reality, and I began to feel like a functioning human being again. David was traveling up to two weeks every month for his job, so it was vital for me to find a workable way to accomplish daily tasks with all three kids in tow.

No outing was simple, of course, but we made it—using the wheelchair for Caroline and sometimes a stroller for Matthew—and nearly always relying on my "little mother," Mary Grace, to supply an extra set of helping hands. From the time Matthew was born, Mary Grace was amazing (I essentially had two babies to take care of for quite a while). She would wake up in the morning and get both of us mentally prepared for the day: "Mommy, where do we need to go today?" Often, since we were constantly running out of things, the schedule included a trip to the grocery store, and we needed to psyche ourselves up for that particular task. I distinctly remember going to bed at night thinking about the dreaded grocery trip the next day and mapping out strategies to minimize the stress.

Mary Grace would ask, "Will you need me to push the wheelchair today, or carry the list and be your runner?" She was an indispensable piece of the complex challenge of shopping for groceries with the Long family, but when Caroline was between the ages of two and five our trip could be made easier if I found the right type of grocery cart waiting when we arrived at the store.

The time when I could put Caroline in the baby seat carts had passed with a blink before we even knew she had Rett Syndrome, but the next type of cart—called amusement carts or fun carts in the retail industry—helped us for a number of years. Amusement carts have attachments for children that are designed to look like fire trucks, racecars, or other fun vehicles, and even though they weren't the safest or most comfortable option for Caroline, I made them work during her preschool years. Those carts, of course, weren't designed for special-needs children, but I didn't have another choice on grocery day.

Amusement carts come in single or double styles, and my first priority was always finding a place for Caroline, who I would carry in on my hip. If we spotted a double amusement cart we hit the mother lode that day, because Matthew could ride next to his sister and Mary Grace could walk and help me find items. If only a single cart was available, Mary Grace would hold Matthew's hand while he toddled along and we would make our way slowly—very slowly—through the store.

This system, although not ideal, worked for us until Caroline was about five years old. As she grew, putting her in the amusement cart became more difficult; she looked like a stuffed sausage. I remember thinking, *This is ridiculous. I'm going to break her leg trying to get her into this cart.* It was at this time I started the new and more complicated maneuver of employing both a wheelchair and a shopping cart on every trip to the store. And the more exhausting the grocery store became—the more I felt like the most overwhelmed customer in any store—the more I looked around at the other cart options with confusion and dismay.

My "a ha!" moment, the epiphany that launched my crazy journey, came when I looked carefully at the baby carts, the amusement carts for toddlers and preschoolers, the electric scooters for people with limited mobility, and the wheelchairs that stores provided for those who needed them. Here was an industry that seemed to bend over backwards to accommodate many types of customers, but I didn't see any type of cart option for an older child or adult with special needs. At first, I convinced myself, I was just missing it. After all, I lived in Alabaster, Alabama (population 31,000), so it was very likely that this special cart had simply not reached my town yet.

So, about 2007, I poured my energy into one quest: finding the cart I needed to simplify my shopping trips.

"I know it must be out there," I told David. "There has to be a special-needs shopping cart. How could there not be?"

Of course, I started on the internet, Googling every combination of words I could think of that might give me the result I was seeking. *Of course it must exist*, I told myself, *I just need to search harder.*

After all, grocery stores have to accommodate people with disabilities, right? They have handicapped parking spaces, handicapped restrooms, graduated curbs for wheelchairs, and electric doors. The abundance of other specialty carts tells me that this is an industry sensitive to the various needs of its customers. So what was I missing? If I could only find the elusive special-needs cart, I told myself I would buy one and donate it to a nearby grocery store and my problem would be solved. I was on it! This would be so easy-peasy.

But no matter how many pages of search results I scrolled through and how I altered the search terms, I came up empty again and again. I love to think about God watching me on this fruitless pursuit, as I pounded the keys on my computer and scrolled, just sure I was going to find it any minute. I imagine Him popping Himself some popcorn and just sitting back to enjoy the search when He knew where it was going to lead, saying to Himself, "Just you wait."

Whenever David traveled to another city, I commissioned him with the task of visiting a grocery store or two to investigate the cart options. And when I was cross-eyed from the Google searches, I started interviewing store managers. It's probably safe to assume that no average mom has chatted with as many grocery store managers as I have over the years. I am sure that they duck into a nearby office when they see me coming!

I would start by introducing Caroline and myself and then I would explain my dilemma. I always gave them a similar spiel.

"You have carts for all ages of children, you have those scooters, you have other handicapped accommodations, and so I'm thinking there must be a cart for older children like Caroline."

I was hoping I would find the one manager with elevated industry knowledge who would say, "Oh, yes, there is a cart like that available! We just have to get on the website and order one!"

Obviously, nothing like that ever happened. Instead, I encountered repeated dead ends, blank stares, and managers saying, "I've never heard of anything like that." Most times they would agree with me wholeheartedly that it should exist, but regrettably, it did not.

I hesitate to use the word "discrimination" too loosely, but the more I explored the world of grocery carts the less I could deny that discrimination was staring right at me.

It would be one thing if grocery stores didn't provide carts at all, of course. But this is an industry known for accommodation, for bending over backwards so that customers have a comfortable and convenient shopping experience. My frustration arose from the fact that grocery stores are typically so obliging, especially to moms shopping with their children. But anyone who is invested in the special-needs community will tell you—and it should go without saying—that you can't make allowances for the able-bodied and not for customers with special needs.

Once, when I was on one of my early research outings at a local store, I talked with the manager about the abundance of options for kids—not just different types of carts but little carts for young children to push, free cookies, family-friendly checkout lanes, sometimes even areas that allow parents to shop while their kids play supervised by store staff. I asked this manager to explain the reason why they purchased amusement carts. He told me, "We have those carts because a happy child equals a happy mom who stays in the store longer and spends more."

As one mom of a child with special needs once told a store manager, "My money is as green as anyone else's." Some retailers don't seem to realize that they have families in their communities with special needs, and the numbers often surprise them. One in five families have a child between the ages of six and eighteen with a special need—physical, emotional, or developmental. Over the years some managers have told me, "We don't have any customers who need a cart like that." My response is always, "They're out there, but you don't see them in your store because it isn't accessible."

Just as a mom of typical children is targeted by grocery stores and given perks so that her children have a good experience, so special-needs families should have the same treatment. As Sara Brewster from Easter Seals said in an early Caroline's Cart brochure, "This shopping cart will make it possible for kids with disabilities to be part of a family shopping outing. More than this, when families use Caroline's Cart in neighborhood stores, it sends an important message to everyone who sees them that kids with disabilities are kids first and need to be included."

Just as much as a cart to ease our shopping experience would be a blessing for our family, we believe it benefits everybody when special-needs kids are included in simple outings and made visible to others in the community. Years after the first seedlings of this need started to push through our consciousness into a full-grown dream, we made a video about Caroline's Cart and David expressed this conviction so well.

"We're here," he said. "We're in your community. Whether you knew us or not, we're here. And so to be able to take your son or daughter, or your elderly loved one with a mobility problem, to the local grocery store, to see other families in the community in that environment—which everybody shares, because everybody goes grocery shopping ... why not see the whole family involved in that?"

For many months, I was digging deep online, approaching store managers, sending David on out-of-state investigations, and using any other outlet I could find to obtain a satisfactory answer to the seemingly simple question that now consumed me: Where was the special-needs shopping cart?

Throughout my quest, I kept up the intense juggling act that was my everyday life, and even though Caroline's myriad health problems had settled down a bit, we were still engaged in regular doctor and hospital visits both for Rett Syndrome and her compromised immune system.

The most significant medical event during this period arose when a team of doctors agreed that we should pursue a bone marrow transplant for Caroline. The pediatric specialists at Children's Hospital of Birmingham referred us to Cincinnati Children's Hospital because of the unique nature of Caroline's blood work. The results of her blood tests were unlike anything they had ever seen, not just because of the extremely low counts but also rare mutations that confounded the doctors. The California experts had already diagnosed her with a cellular immunodeficiency, but through further tests, specialists told us that Caroline had "zero natural killer cells," among other deficiencies, which explained her extreme vulnerability to viruses she came near.

The visit to Cincinnati launched our preparation for the transplant, and our circle of friends and family started a campaign to help us raise money for the procedure. It was a whirlwind. We were well down that path—four-year-old Matthew was a match and we had decided he would be the donor—when the stem cell unit in Cincinnati determined that the risk of transplant was too great and Caroline probably wouldn't survive it. So as quickly as we were planning for a transplant, that option was off the table. Here is an excerpt from the letter the stem cell specialists sent us on October 30 of that year:

> This seven-year-old with Rett has unfortunately also apparently inherited a selective defect in her viral killing capacity, primarily through an almost total lack of function of her natural killer cells. However, after due consideration our stem cell unit felt that risk of transplant weighed against her uncertain risk of severe illness did not warrant going through with the transplant.

Every consultation offered more information about the medical puzzle that was our daughter, but in truth very little had changed in our lives—except I was increasingly obsessed with the absence of an accessible shopping cart and the unsettling feeling that I might be called to address that need.

All men dream, but not equally.
Those who dream by night in the
dusty recesses of their minds, wake
in the day to find that it was vanity:
but the dreamers of the day are
dangerous men, for they may act on
their dreams with open eyes, to make
them possible.

T. E. Lawrence

4

Dog on a Bone

I AM NOT TYPICALLY KNOWN for persistence or an iron-clad work ethic. But as months turned into a year of fruitless searching for a special-needs cart, David was struck by my tenacity. As I heard him describe it to a friend one day, "Drew isn't always known for her follow-through. She's very laid-back, and she doesn't worry about the house being spotless or a project staying unfinished. But she's like a dog on a bone with this special-needs cart. I've never seen her like this."

Throughout 2008, I was thinking about the lack of a special-needs cart nearly all of the time. I went to sleep with it on my mind, woke up frustrated about it, and prayed about it often enough to become convinced I had heard God deliver a pretty startling message, and that message was to move forward with the cart. Our lives were so chaotic that I didn't rush to drop the bombshell on David until we had some time to ourselves—and that was a rare occurrence indeed. Fortunately, in mid-November David arranged for my mom to keep our children (she had moved up to Alabaster after Hurricane Katrina flooded her home in Louisiana) and surprised me with a trip to Nashville in honor of my fortieth birthday.

We had only been on the road for a little while when I spilled the beans with the statement that would define the next decade or more of our lives.

"I really feel like the Lord has laid it on my heart to design a special-needs grocery cart."

He looked at me as pointedly as someone could while driving on the interstate.

"You want to do it?" he asked.

"Well, why *not* me?" I responded.

"Well, *why* you?" he shot back.

As our conversation proceeded, I reiterated my frustration at the lack of accommodation for children like Caroline and my strong conviction that I was supposed to do something about it—something that would honor our daughter. He asked all of the right questions—I was, after all, neither an engineer nor a millionaire, and everything about this was crazy on its face. I ended up asking him to do one thing: pray.

It was my birthday weekend, and we had Thanksgiving and Christmas coming up, a jam-packed season for any family. I asked David to pray about it over the next six or seven weeks, until school resumed after the holidays. David is a godly man, and if he says he will pray about something he isn't just paying lip service. I told him that we wouldn't talk about it anymore until January, but I would be back to him then to see what he had heard from the Lord.

We agreed on that plan, but I know I brought up the cart at least once more that weekend, while we were eating at a restaurant. I drew my first rudimentary sketch of the cart on a napkin, and I know I said something like "See? How hard can it be?"

As it turned out, that was a rhetorical question to which I truly didn't want the answer, but in those early days my naiveté worked to my advantage. As I thought through what little I could imagine about chasing this idea, it just didn't seem all that complicated. I was fond of telling David, "It's not a rocket ship!" It might not have been a rocket ship but it was plenty complicated—a fact that was revealed to me in mercifully small doses in the coming months and years.

Fast forward to January 7, 2009. The holidays were now behind us and all three of the kids had gone back to their respective schools—Mary Grace and Matthew to Evangel Classical Christian School and Caroline to the Alabaster public schools. David had a home office on the bottom floor of our house, and when I had returned home after driving everyone to school I walked down there and sat across from him.

"Have you been praying about it?" I asked him.

"Yes."

"What are your thoughts?"

"I am one hundred percent for it. I feel like the Lord has said, 'We need to try this.' I will support you, I'll be your cheerleader, I'll do what I can, but it's going to have to fall on you."

David has played numerous roles through the development and marketing of Caroline's Cart, but cheerleader has certainly been one of the most consistent and crucial. He has supported and encouraged me, but he has always reminded me that this was *my* calling and *my* burden. Another vital part he has played in this drama is that of a steadying force. I tend to fly between emotional extremes—either overly enthusiastic, pie-in-the-sky, full-speed-ahead with no perspective when things are going well, or in tearful despair when I hit an obstacle. His job is to keep me moving and keep me centered between those two extremes. It's not an easy job, I can assure you.

David has never wavered in his support of the cart or me. He has worked in the college loan industry for more than twenty years, but right about the time we first discussed Caroline's Cart President Obama announced a complete overhaul of college student lending that essentially eliminated private loan companies from the equation. Suddenly David was worried about his job security, and he thought that if the cart was successful, it could provide a safety net if his income dried up.

He told people that I talked about the cart so incessantly that he told me to do something about it or quit talking about it. Guilty! No one has ever accused me of being timid or soft-spoken, and when I have a strong opinion about something you will most definitely know it. In those days, my chief topic of conversation was a special-needs cart, and my most frequent captive audiences were David and Shrek, Caroline's favorite character from her favorite movie. Her stuffed Shrek doll went everywhere with us, so I vented to that ogre pretty often.

After David told me he was on board and asked that fateful question—"What are you going to do about it?"—I raced back upstairs. I was so excited. I grabbed a piece of paper and a pen, sat down at my dining room table, and drew my second sketch of the cart. This one was better than the rough draft on the napkin from the restaurant—more detailed and more inspiring because it represented the start of something that was really happening.

I was so proud of my drawing I could hardly contain it. I ran back downstairs—David shooing me away while he tried to conduct a conference call—and waved it around in his face.

"See? It's so simple! I told you, it's not a rocket ship!"

When he was able to reply, he answered me in his unflappable way again: "Great. Now what are you going to do next?"

Back up the stairs I trotted with my drawing in my hand, and I stopped dead in the middle of the kitchen floor. What *was* I going to do next? The emotion of that moment was thrilling. I know it sounds stupid, but I felt such a sense of accomplishment. I had something on a piece of paper—I had started! I finally had a concrete goal and, in that moment, clueless about the pitfalls that awaited me, I had no doubt about the success of my fictional cart.

I sat down and turned on my laptop. For a long time I just stared at the screen. What in the world should I even search for? "How to design a grocery cart"? "Creating a new product"? Instinctively, I knew those phrases weren't going to yield the concrete steps I was seeking. I jumped up and stuck my head back down the stairs where David had probably just managed to get himself focused on his day job again after my last interruption.

"David, I don't even know what to Google!"

"I don't know, you probably need some kind of engineer to tell you if this will even work!"

I seized on this idea and grabbed the Birmingham telephone book. An engineer might know how to help me move from a sketch on a piece of paper to a cart that one could actually push through a grocery store. I opened up the Yellow Pages to the *E* section and started calling local engineering firms. It was the first time I had tried to explain my curious quest to an outsider, and I found myself stumbling a bit to articulate what I needed. My telephone speech that winter went something like this:

"Hi, I know this is going to sound really weird, but I didn't know if there was someone there who could help me. I'm just a mom, I live in Alabaster, so I'm local, and I am trying to design a product—a shopping cart for people with special needs. I just didn't know if you worked with people like me or if there was someone I could come talk to about it."

I probably called between ten and fifteen engineering firms and delivered some variation on this little speech. A few people let me know quickly that they couldn't help me and ended the conversation with haste. Others were slightly curious and inquired about the cart I had envisioned, but none of them had the means or desire to even set up a meeting with me. It stung a little bit to hear the word "no" over and over from those engineering companies, but it was a good warm-up for the flurry of rejections to come.

My days ended at one o'clock when Matthew finished preschool, so soon it was time to put the phone book away and head to the carpool line. Even when things started happening and the to-do list associated with the cart grew, I worked on it when I had the time and space, and that was seldom more than a few hours a day. When Caroline wasn't at school, she was a full-time job. On top of that, Mary Grace was starting to have dance class several times a week, Matthew was playing T-ball, and there was the endless cycle of grocery shopping, preparing meals, doing laundry, and cleaning the house. Eventually it would be hard to fit everything in, but that January I was still looking for the next step that would move me down the road toward an actual cart.

That night at dinner, I recounted my day for my family and lamented the lack of response from Birmingham's engineering community. David made his best suggestion so far.

"Why don't you call UAB?"

The University of Alabama at Birmingham, a sprawling research-based public university, sat about thirty minutes from my front door and offered a host of academic programs and, David theorized, possibly an engineering student in search of a senior design project. At the very least, it was the type of institution where people might take the time to answer questions and offer direction.

The next time I had the opportunity, I started trying to reach the right person at UAB. I probably talked to fifty people within the university system before I finally connected with a friendly woman in the engineering department who listened to my whole story. As had become my habit, I asked if I might come in and meet with someone there, and my heart soared when she said, "Yes, I can probably make you an appointment with Dr. Soni. He's the head of the mechanical engineering department, and he might be helpful to you."

This was the most thrilling moment so far. I had an appointment! I wrote the February date and the time on my calendar and called out to David, who was working in his home office, breathless with my news. My mission had started out haltingly, but with this trip to UAB I was hopeful that the pieces were starting to click into place.

Faith sees the invisible,
believes the unbelievable,
and receives the impossible.

Corrie ten Boom

5

R & D

MY APPOINTMENT AT UAB WAS set for 9:00 one February morning with Dr. Bharat Soni. I knew nothing about him except what the receptionist had told me when she arranged the meeting—that he was the head of the mechanical engineering department at the university. I dropped off the kids at their respective schools, parked in the lot outside the engineering building, took a deep breath, and bowed my head. "Lord, please either open this door or close it," I prayed. "Here I am. I've prayed for this meeting, and the next step is up to You."

I entered the building, praying the whole time for courage, announced myself to the lady at the desk, and soon found myself sitting across from Dr. Soni, a somber academic type who greeted me politely. Once we were seated in his office, I launched into my presentation again—*I'm just a mom from Alabaster who saw a need ... I feel strongly that this cart should exist but I don't know how to make it happen ... I'm just trying to help special-needs families but I really need some direction.*

He sat there stone-faced while I rambled, listening but offering me little encouragement. “Oh Lord,” I was thinking, “I asked You for a closed door and it seems to be slamming right in my face, only a month after I started this journey.” But when I stopped talking and gave him a chance to respond, the mood in the room changed completely.

Dr. Soni told me that he had an adult son with special needs, a young man who would spend his whole life in a wheelchair and would have benefited greatly from Caroline’s Cart if it had been available in his younger years. He told me that his wife had expressed her own frustration about the difficulty of grocery shopping many times, and they had wondered together whether there was an easier way. He said to me pointedly, “This cart needs to happen. It’s a good idea, and you need to pursue it.”

His encouragement was like oxygen to me, but he couldn’t offer me much in the way of practical help. He told me I just missed the deadline for senior design projects and there was a waiting list anyway, so that route would only slow me down. He didn’t offer to send me to someone who could build the grocery cart, but he did prove himself my ally, and his vote of confidence gave me an unbelievable boost. With this fellow special-needs parent, an intelligent man with knowledge of product design, the Lord had made it clear to me that this door needed to stay wide open for now. As I left there, I was so exhilarated. It was like I had been on the long journey to Oz, and I had finally seen the Wizard.

When I got back into my van after the meeting, I started sobbing. I was beside myself. I can't really explain why that moment was so emotional, except for the fact that God had answered my prayer in a very personal, pointed way by putting Dr. Soni in my path, and I was buoyed with renewed energy and faith in my cause.

I called David and tried to explain why I was crying. I told him about my uplifting conversation with Dr. Soni.

"What can they do for you?" he asked me.

"Well, nothing," I answered, "but I think the whole purpose of that meeting was to encourage me!"

Of course, the next time I sat at my laptop I was back to the drawing board, but slowly my next step was starting to click into focus. I needed an actual model of Caroline's Cart, a prototype, so that I could promote it to families and stores. A prototype would allow me to measure the interest I knew would be out there, and if I generated enthusiasm, pretty soon I would be taking actual orders for carts. Even with a few snags, I was still convinced at this point that we could be taking and fulfilling orders in six months—a year at the most.

I couldn't have possibly been more clueless.

Every morning I sat at the kitchen table and made phone calls to more design firms—but this time I knew I was looking for companies that specialized in product design or prototypes. Even with this refined focus, most of the conversations were discouragingly short. My goal, with every contact, was to get past the receptionist to an actual engineer. Maybe I would find the next Dr. Soni—another person who embraced my idea; and maybe he or she could tell me how to turn it into an actual shopping cart.

Matthew was attending preschool three mornings a week during this time, so he was home with me for much of that first year. He was just four years old, but soon he and I designated ourselves as the official Caroline's Cart R & D (research and development) team—and we took our task seriously. When I had a few hours to myself I would make phone calls or search for engineering leads on the computer, and when Matthew was with me we spent hours visiting area stores and learning everything we could about shopping carts.

After we dropped off Caroline and Mary Grace at school, I would plot our course—as far as we could get from Alabaster to do thorough research and then make it back to the carpool line for the 2:30 pickup. Matthew didn't work for free—he usually got a Sprite and a pack of Skittles out of the deal, so he was a pretty big fan of this assignment. As he got older and the cart finally took hold he was always proud of his role in helping lay the foundation when he was just a preschooler.

Once we got inside, we could pull a shopping cart from the bay and wheel it to the back of the store, where I would promptly flip it over, take a few pictures of it, and pull my tape measure out of my purse. Then I would measure it and examine its workmanship and any special features that might be relevant. Have you ever looked at the underside of a grocery cart? Neither had I. I had no idea what I was even looking for, but it made me feel better to be doing *something.* Every once in a while a store employee would come along looking puzzled at the sight of this crazy lady and her cute son studying an upside-down grocery cart. Because I had become a regular at chatting about my cart idea with store employees, I launched into my speech and told them why we had invaded their store.

The information we gathered on those trips was invaluable later when we got serious about design and manufacturing, and our careful inspection yielded another clue that would one day be the most important piece of the puzzle. Most of the carts, especially those in stores belonging to large chains, had the word "Technibilt" stamped on the underside. That was the first time I had encountered Technibilt, but before long that one company would hold the keys to the cart's success.

Another important step I took in 2009 wasn't nearly as much fun as R & D with Matthew (and much more costly than Sprite and Skittles). We knew it was time to hire a local attorney to help ensure legal protection through the development of the cart. We also contacted a patent attorney to help me navigate the thorny and expensive world of patent procurement.

The first attorney I hired, Brad Anderson (now with a Birmingham firm called Butler Snow), became both friend and advisor in those early days. By the following year he would walk me through the formation of our company, give direction regarding a patent attorney, and keep me alert to the many legal pitfalls that can trap an entrepreneur.

From my kitchen table that spring and summer, I chased down engineering firms across the nation for six months (there went my original timetable!) before coming across an Indianapolis-based company called Indesign. I remember thinking, *I've called everybody else in the world, why not call this one too?* Many months of dead-end phone calls had yielded at least one upside—I had improved the delivery of my "elevator speech." I had become more polished and professional, identifying myself as an entrepreneur with an idea instead of "just a mom from Alabaster, Alabama." And that day in late 2009, on the phone with Indesign, my little speech gave me a small victory—a transfer from the receptionist to a manager named Griffin Bryce.

I was past the receptionist! Finally I had the ear of a bona fide project manager, and I just about talked that ear off as I spilled the story of the birth of the Caroline's Cart idea and the rocky road I had traveled so far in an effort to give the cart some credibility. Later Mr. Bryce told me that he didn't know if he would ever get me off the phone. I don't think I came up for air—I just spilled my story like I was scared that if I paused he would end the conversation. He listened, explained that even though Indesign specializes in electrical engineering they also employ some mechanical engineers who might be able to tackle a project like mine, and concluded by telling me he would talk to the CEO and call me back.

That small breakthrough became a wide-open explosion a few days later, when Mr. Bryce called me back and told me Indesign was interested in producing my prototype! As a first step, he said, we would talk through my idea thoroughly in a series of phone calls, and from those calls they would create scale 2-D drawings of the cart. After the drawings were completed to my satisfaction, they would start building the actual prototype.

Those drawings weren't cheap, and I only had conference calls as a means to move the concept that was in my brain onto a piece of paper in Indianapolis. I remember being terrified that they wouldn't understand my descriptions of the cart's features, that the drawings would come and they would be all wrong.

The first official design for Caroline's Cart came to our house via UPS in February 2010, thirteen months after I sat down at my dining room table and made my first sketch. It was one 8½″ x 11″ card that represented so much more, and when I pulled it out of the box I just started sobbing.

I cried because I knew we were taking a huge step, and also because they had understood me, and I was looking at my cart, professionally rendered. I remember running downstairs to David's home office, holding the drawing in front of his face, and seeing his mouth fall open. Not only did we have something tangible to hold and show people, the receipt of the drawing meant that Indesign was ready to start work on our prototype.

Of course, as kind and accommodating as the Indesign engineers were, their expertise came at a price, so that winter marked the first time I had to write a large check (four figures, taken from our savings account) in the interest of the cart. It was the beginning of a terrifying four-year period characterized by a one-way cash flow; I wrote countless checks from our hard-earned savings in pursuit of an expensive dream with no early promise that a dime of it would come back. Call it faith or insanity, but with every expenditure our commitment to the cart grew commensurately.

It had been more than a year since David and I agreed that God was giving us the green light to move forward on the cart. In that time, I had little to show for it physically except a very nice—and very expensive—drawing. But the knowledge I had gleaned from countless conversations with store managers, engineers, friends, family members, and others had been enough to educate me about the product development process and keep me on this winding road, encouraged and hopeful and blissfully unaware of the snares that still awaited me.

You have been assigned this
mountain to show others
it can be moved.

Unknown

6

The Desert

BECAUSE OF THAT ONE BEAUTIFUL drawing on card stock, my confidence in the cart project was soaring. I was finally moving the ball, and if I ever doubted it I could just gaze at that card and dream about the places it would lead.

From our investigative R & D trips the previous year, Matthew and I had determined that Technibilt was an important company in the grocery cart industry. I researched the company and learned that "important" was an understatement. Technibilt, based in Newton, North Carolina, is North America's leading shopping cart manufacturer and the distributor for virtually every national retail chain. Convinced that the road would have to go through Technibilt, I called them for the first time in February 2010. They get tons of these calls every week, so I was fortunate when they eventually returned my call.

The man who called me back was Alan Deal, Technibilt's plant manager. He would eventually become one of my most steadfast supporters in that company over the years. Alan listened and suggested that I come to North Carolina to talk in more detail, and eventually we selected June 14 for David and me to go up there. I can't overstate how huge it was that I even had a meeting with Technibilt written in ink in my planner. While I waited for that meeting, I also made contact with a well-known organization that would eventually lend its name to the cart and give us a huge boost in national credibility—Easter Seals.

We had been connected with Easter Seals for most of Caroline's life, and we valued the organization's persistence and success in lobbying for families with special needs. Late in 2009 we had received word that Caroline was selected as the organization's 2010 National Ambassador, and as the recipient of that honor Caroline and our family had the opportunity to travel to several Easter Seals events, including national conventions in Chicago and Washington, D.C., and a gathering of their donors in San Diego. As I sought ways to elevate the profile of my cart proposal, Easter Seals was one of the first connections I pursued.

I was hoping that Easter Seals and Caroline's Cart could support each other, since we serve the same population, and I asked if we could put the familiar Easter Seals lily logo on the seat of each cart. I knew that a seal of approval from the largest disability services organization on the planet would give us cachet that nothing else could touch. Through an early conference call with Easter Seals representatives and a live meeting with David in the Chicago office in March, we arrived at an understanding that would go into effect when we actually had some carts.

Seven years after that first meeting, the cart still proudly carries the Easter Seals logo.

If we ever had carts on which to display the logo, I was confident that the Easter Seals support would be a crucial piece of our marketing puzzle. But as excited as I was about the feedback we had received from Easter Seals, it was a little bit like putting the cart before the horse (no pun intended). I had never pushed or touched an actual Caroline's Cart—despite the considerable investment we had already made—because none existed.

One of the first directives my attorney Brad Anderson had given me was to form a company as the umbrella organization for Caroline's Cart, and by March of 2010 I was officially the founder and president of Parent Solution Group LLC, or PSG. With the new credibility afforded me by PSG, I also filed both U.S. and international patent applications—and each one of those required me to write another check. I was completely unprepared for the mounting expense required to lay the groundwork for a new product. Everything cost a lot of money, and at times I really didn't even know exactly where the money was going. One of my attorneys would tell me a check was required, and I was compelled to write it or risk sabotaging the process.

If the financial strain wasn't enough, we were suddenly faced with another medical trial as well. Our Rett's specialist in Birmingham had told us that hip and back problems often surface in girls who have the disorder, and in early 2010, as I drowned in patent forms and incorporation papers, we learned that Caroline would need surgery that summer to stabilize her hip. The surgery was scheduled for July, just weeks after David and I were to take the road trip to our much-anticipated appointment at the Technibilt plant in North Carolina. I had been sick in bed just before the trip, but I rallied because I knew how important this was and I was afraid that if I canceled I would never get another shot with Technibilt.

When we pulled into the company parking lot, I was nervous but incredibly excited. I had put this company on such a pedestal, even though at that point I still didn't know the degree to which they dominated the grocery cart industry. Like I had done before the UAB meeting sixteen months earlier, David and I bowed our heads when we pulled into the parking lot and prayed: "Lord, please guide us through this meeting. We know that this journey either really gets started today or it ends today."

We spent several hours with Alan Deal, who at long last, gave us the perspective of a shopping cart industry insider. We handed him our professional 2-D drawings and gave him the highlights and the lowlights of the journey so far, and we held our breath as we waited for his verdict. It was remarkably similar to the response I received from Dr. Soni at UAB—wholehearted encouragement but not the partnership we were seeking.

Alan loved the idea, he told us, and he didn't know why no one had ever come up with it before. He knew grocery carts as well as anybody in the world, and he urged us to continue to move forward with the prototype and marketing efforts and promised to talk with some of his colleagues to see if Technibilt could become involved. He also delivered the shocking reality that the checks I had been writing at that point—checks that had depleted our life savings—were just chump change compared to what a cart could cost. He told me that the labor and machinery required to make a custom injection mold for a plastic cart was incredibly expensive. For my design, he estimated that it would cost about a million dollars to bring the cart to market. I'm sure I stopped breathing.

We certainly didn't have a closed door when we left that day, but for a number of months we heard very little from them. I would find out later that the firm was in the process of being acquired by a larger company, which made it difficult for them to pull the trigger on something new with questionable profit potential. I was still hopeful, but I had to come back down to earth in record time and return to mommy mode when we got back to Alabama, because it was time to check Caroline into the hospital for her surgery.

If the weeks after Matthew's birth felt like a wilderness period, the summer of 2010 was a trek through the driest of deserts. We didn't have an answer from Technibilt, and to add to that uncertainty the drastic changes in David's industry came home to roost with the stunning news that he had been laid off. (We received that seismic news just two days before the surgery). We weren't completely surprised, but because we were going out on so many limbs in obedience to the Lord we thought He certainly wouldn't chop down the tree right out from under us. David's salary was what allowed us to make a mortgage payment, keep the lights on, buy groceries, and keep me in sweet tea and M&M's while I chased what still looked like an improbable dream. I felt lightheaded, like someone had knocked the air out of me, when he told me the news. Then I remember David asking me, "Are we going to lose our house?"

Alabama summers are hot enough, but that summer in the "desert" was nearly unbearable. After a week in the hospital, I spent seven weeks caring for Caroline as she recovered from her hip surgery (in a full hot-pink body cast), crying out to God about His will for my family, the cart, David's job, and this abrupt dead end we seemed to be facing. I stopped making phone calls about the cart and just read business books and inspirational stories about people of faith and entrepreneurs who had succeeded against the odds.

I read about James Dyson, who was dissatisfied with the way typical vacuum cleaners worked but still went through five years and countless prototypes before inventing the first bagless vacuum. (By the way, I have a Dyson and it's the best vacuum I've ever owned, and I'm not being paid to say that!) I learned about the development of Post-it notes—seen as "a solution without a problem" for years until a colleague of the inventor began to use them to save his place in his hymnal (and now we all wonder how we ever lived without them!).

And I drew courage from the story I heard of a mom who had great success with her own innovation for the shopping cart—a padded cover for the seat that protects babies and toddlers from germs and provides them a more comfortable ride.

With every article I read about a great idea and the inventor who brought it to the marketplace, I became more convinced that, despite the hurdles that seemed to be multiplying in my path, Caroline's Cart had a glimmer of a chance to succeed. The need was obvious, and it existed in an industry that prided itself in providing service to a wide range of customers. I just had to figure out a way to make the carts and then convince stores that they needed to purchase them.

Unlike most entrepreneurs, I had the added headache of inventing a product that is sold only to retailers. When the typical entrepreneur creates a new product and a retailer decides to stock it, the retailer can mark up the price, both parties make a profit, and everyone is happy. There are all sorts of books giving advice on how to sell a widget to Walmart, but I was like an entrepreneur who was trying to create and sell a better type of shelf to hold the widget. Shopping carts are a cost of doing business for a grocer, not something they sell, and they don't provide an immediate payoff for the store. Understandably, in a low-margin business like the retail food industry, a new capital expenditure (like, say, a new type of shopping cart) represents a risk.

I learned early in my research that most stores have a policy forbidding parents from bringing their own carts to do their shopping. So even if I were able to produce the carts and launch a dynamic marketing blitz on social media, the families that needed them most wouldn't be able to buy and use them. I was absolutely beholden to the retail grocery industry and to their suppliers, and on top of that tangled web I was facing the prospect of mounting bills with no source of income. As hard as I searched, I didn't find a single story of an entrepreneur who had done what I was trying to do—sell to the retailer rather than the consumer.

All that was left of Caroline's Cart was a sliver of hope and that very nice professional drawing. My momentum was dead. I couldn't possibly spend another dime on this pipe dream. I might not have been pursuing leads on the cart, but I was going stir-crazy in the house, and air conditioning was a requirement for any outing. So regularly I would pack up Caroline in her body cast and take her to Target, which was new in Alabaster. We went at least twice a week, with me pushing Caroline in a special wheelchair designed for people in body casts, and it was a mindless activity that allowed me to put one foot in front of the other even as my cart journey seemed to be skidding to a halt.

During this time, we were praying fervently but feeling hopeless. I distinctly remember, at least once that summer, David suggesting that it might be time to cut our losses and give up on Caroline's Cart. David filed for unemployment to keep some cash coming in, and we waited for his company to hand down a severance package that we guessed would cover, at best, two months' salary. We had taken a leap of faith, and it looked like we were heading for a devastating fall.

Many are the plans
in the mind of a man,
but it is the purpose of the LORD
that will stand.

Proverbs 19:21

7

Creative Provision

THIS WAS THE LONG DEFINITION of family fun in the summer of 2010: a child in a full body cast, an unemployed husband, two other children asking if we could go on vacation, Matthew requesting a superhero theme for his sixth-birthday party, bills coming in from attorneys, and the looming question of where the money for a prototype could possibly come from. If I had been the picture of the naive rookie entrepreneur when we started this journey, I was now slamming into the sheer rock face of reality, and I wondered in earnest if my crazy idea had reached its conclusion.

Through the weeks by Caroline's bedside after her surgery and after we returned home, I stepped back from the cart emotionally because I had too many stressors vying for attention in my life. So many times, I would lie down next to Caroline and cry. I would ask her to pray for me, and I would cry out to God with the most raw and honest prayer I had ever prayed in my life—asking Him to shed some light on what seemed like an impossibly dark situation. Everything was on hold during those months except the absolute necessities for my family, and I remember telling the Lord that, for the moment, I just couldn't handle the cart; He would have to hold it for me for a while.

But God intended to put it back in my hands, and with a dramatic flair. Early in the fall, after the humbling experience of depositing David's first unemployment check, he finally received notice outlining his severance package. Instead of the two months' pay we were expecting, the severance check was for more than a year's salary! We were so stunned that we thought it must have been a misprint, and David called his former company to make sure the amount was correct.

It was no mistake, and almost as soon as we had absorbed the enormity of that blessing we received another one when David got another job with a company in the same industry. Suddenly the lowest time in our lives so far—the rampant fear and regret over the money that we had already spent on the cart project, the confusion over whether God really had given us this calling—turned into a celebration of His creative provision.

We were nearing an even more expensive season in the life of the cart—one that would cost five figures just for a prototype—and in retrospect we would never have been able to see it through if not for that unexpectedly large severance check. The Lord turned our most desolate storm into one of our greatest encouragements as it dawned on us that if David hadn't been laid off we might not have secured the money we needed to continue. My hope was renewed, and I was ready to take on the next step. Cheered by this development, I called Indesign that fall and told them I was ready to begin the prototype.

That November, I received a twelve-page packet known as a "Statement of Work" that detailed the concept of the cart—features like a five-point harness restraint, handles that rotate in and out to make it easier to place someone in the seat, and a one-piece molded seat that would face the person pushing the cart. I remember thinking, *Twelve pages? Are you serious? It's not a rocket ship!* But I can tell you it had a rocket ship price tag—close to $25,000. But it was money well-spent: With a few modifications, that initial proposal mirrored the cart that would eventually aid special-needs families all over the world.

Before the construction of the prototype could officially begin Indesign gave me a task to complete. (After searching for direction for so long, it was a tremendous relief for someone else to give me a job!) In a trend that was becoming predictable, the assignment was much more complicated than I ever imagined it would be. The engineers at Indesign needed an actual shopping cart to guide them in their project, and they asked me to get my hands on one and have it shipped to Indianapolis. I was ready to pay for a used shopping cart and I wasn't picky about which store it came from, but still I encountered one refusal after another.

Whether it's an issue of liability or the fear of their brand name being misused, retailers are unyielding in their refusal to sell a used cart to an entrepreneurial mom from Alabama or anyone else. My favorite encounter came with a sympathetic employee from a Home Depot not too far from my home, who listened to my story and then advised me, "You know, sometimes shopping carts get left out at night, and if someone were to come by when we were closed and put one in their truck, we really wouldn't be the wiser."

So, it was fine to *steal* their shopping cart, but they couldn't *sell* me one? It was truly tempting, but after careful consideration and a little bit of fun with David imagining how we would pull off the proposed late-night larceny, we decided that if God was calling us to make the cart a reality we would do it the right way or risk losing His blessing. Stealing was not an option.

Back to Google I went, where I finally found a company in Maine that specialized in refurbished shopping carts. They were willing to sell me one and send it to Indianapolis. Finally the engineers had something to guide them as they worked.

In early 2011, with the plans approved and in hand, they got to work on the first Caroline's Cart. And in one of the more obvious God-ordained events in a long chain of them, my husband's new company was headquartered in Indianapolis and he was required to travel there at least once a month.

David became my eyes on the ground to watch the prototype take shape, and he checked in with the Indesign staff as needed. It was killing me that he got to see it progress and I didn't. He would take photos and call me to give a report, but that wasn't the same as being there. The engineers and I talked on the phone fairly frequently, and they too sent me pictures from time to time.

As we kept tabs on that project, I also met a group of people who gave me a different kind of boost. My attorney suggested that I meet with the people at Innovation Depot in Birmingham, a business incubator designed to aid technology efforts, startups, and entrepreneurs with mentors, funds, and other forms of support. I called and scheduled a time to meet with Devon Laney, then the vice president of Innovation Depot, and he introduced me to Dennis Leonard, a former general manager of several television stations and an entrepreneur with experience and connections. He loved the cart, and he sprung into action trying to line up some support for me.

Soon Dennis and I were meeting with Darlene Rotch, a public relations executive I met through Innovation Depot who lent us valuable marketing expertise in those early days. Rebel Negley, Darlene's senior vice president at her PR firm, would later become a crucial player in this story. Rebel was sitting in on the meeting, and my story made an impression on her. The PR firm used to meet people all the time, people who had an idea they wanted to promote. But when I came in, she told me later, "I had chills, literal chills." She turned around and told an associate, "You just met the next most successful woman, because that is going to be huge."

At Dennis's urging, we created the Caroline's Cart team—consisting of Dennis, Darlene, my attorney Brad Anderson, his colleague Randy McClanahan, and myself.

We started to meet every couple of months or so to map out strategies for business development, funding, and marketing. Collaboration with that team convinced me that what I was doing had a real shot of succeeding, and through their connections and advice I developed a business plan and started to get some media exposure in the Birmingham area.

When I didn't have any idea what the next step was, my team encouraged me and guided me along paths that had worked in their own lives or in the lives of other entrepreneurs they knew. Sometimes we hit some home runs in our collaboration and other times we struck out, but it was good to have others sharing the journey for a change.

There were others too—people in the grocery cart industry or other businesses who stepped in when I most needed a shot of encouragement. One of those coaches was Gene Cary, who had built his Birmingham business from the ground up making refrigeration units for grocery stores. Because my entrepreneurial path was so much more complicated than most of the people I had read about that summer, contact with someone else who had produced and marketed units for grocery stores was invaluable. Gene was generous with his time and business wisdom throughout my journey. He had me over often for coffee, and in those meetings he would answer all of my questions and even pray with me.

In those early years I was so desperate for guidance that I would take off down any road suggested by someone with more business experience than me (which was just about everybody). In retrospect, I spent some money and time that truly didn't advance the cart, but I didn't know any better. I was so clueless. There were seasons, before I had the prototype, when I pursued ideas and leads simply because doing something was better than doing nothing, and I didn't know which path might lead to an unexpected success.

Throughout early 2011, the team of engineers was still steadily working in their Indianapolis workshop, building the prototype that would finally give Caroline's Cart the stamp of legitimacy. I love to think about them tinkering around, coming up with the plans and processes that would make the cart as functional and efficient as possible. They would send me pictures of their progress periodically, and every picture brought the day a little closer when I could actually push the cart that I had first sketched on a napkin and then imagined and dreamed about countless times.

As I waited for the prototype, the other saga that seemed endless was the elusive pursuit of patents. U.S. and international patents have separate applications and separate approval protocols, and nothing about the process is streamlined, simple, or cheap. It's a grueling undertaking requiring the inventor to spend thousands and thousands and thousands of dollars, and your patent might not even get issued. You could spend a hundred thousand dollars in legal fees, file all the right documents, and there's absolutely no guarantee your patent will get issued. It happens all the time. It's all in the hands of one person who works at the patent office, and they can make a subjective decision that one product is too similar to another and refuse the application. My U.S. design patent was issued in 2010, and the international patents came through, but the utility patent—the one that covers the cart itself—could take years.

Throughout that winter, I tried to keep the Caroline's Cart plates spinning and also scrambled like crazy to take care of the needs of my family. I was back in my normal multitasking rhythm, beyond grateful that the hope of the cart was still alive after the most harrowing year of my life. I understood at this point that I really was in this for the long haul, and I believed fervently that some significant breakthroughs were on the way.

If you can dream it, you can do it.

Walt Disney (attributed)

8

The Prototype

AS ONE WINTER DAY RAN into another, I was living for the moment when I would get the phone call from Indesign letting me know the prototype was finally complete. I was still meeting with my team, but we reached a point where we decided we really couldn't do anything more until we got the prototype. So we waited.

To fill the time, I worried about the cart's prospects once we did actually have one we could push around. My extensive research of other entrepreneurs and their paths had convinced me that a mom from Alabaster trying to create and sell a product to retailers was both unprecedented and probably insane. I would vent to David (and Shrek) about it.

"All of these other people sell to the consumer. No one that I know of has ever done this before. What am I thinking? What if no one buys it or I can't even get an audience with the grocery chains?"

Always the steadying force, David would tell me, "You don't even have a prototype yet, sister. Calm down.

You're on step six thousand, and you should be on step two hundred."

Then in late February 2011 a phone number popped up on my screen with an Indianapolis area code. On the other end was an Indesign engineer telling me I was free to drive up there anytime to pick up my completed prototype! I wanted to just jump in the car and take off right then and there, but that was unheard of at that stage of my life. Before I could even think of leaving town, I had to do hours of preparation—writing out Caroline's medicine and therapy schedule, Matthew's T-ball schedule, and Mary Grace's dance schedule for David; washing school uniforms; arranging rides with neighbors; and making sure everyone was straight on homework and projects.

I recruited my sister Pam to join me for the trip. We took the back seats out of my van to make room for the cart, and we headed for points north. I know I was a ball of jumpy excitement all the way up to Indiana, and at some level I really couldn't believe it was happening. We checked into a hotel on March 1, ready to get up bright and early the next morning to drive to the Indesign office.

When I think about the emotions of that morning, on our way to Indesign, and when I first laid my hands on the prototype, I feel like the English language doesn't have sufficient words to describe the way I felt. I was about to lay eyes on something I had been talking about, praying about, agonizing over, and dreaming of for years. Those years had been marked by plenty of setbacks and we almost abandoned the cart altogether, but that morning every trial, every discouragement, seemed to evaporate. It was a tremendous feeling of accomplishment to know we finally had a prototype, but also humility that God had actually let us get this far. I felt boundless gratitude and joy, even as I had this surreal feeling that I was watching someone else in my body.

We arrived at Indesign, got our visitors' badges, exchanged pleasantries, and were ushered into a room where we were told that the cart was just on the other side of the wall. After what seemed like forever (but was really only about a minute), they walked us into a large room, and there she was, in all her three-dimensional glory—an actual Caroline's Cart! I was speechless. I felt like I was looking at my fourth baby, and I certainly had the labor pains and the scars to show for it. The cart that greeted us on March 2, 2011, was very similar to the one that today helps thousands of special-needs families have an accessible shopping experience. It was painted a light orange color, with a gray seat and handles that swung out to make it easier to put a passenger into the seat and then pivoted back together when it was time to push the cart. It had a five-point harness, a basket behind the seat for groceries, and a tray on the bottom to hold more items.

One of the first things I did was sit in the cart to try it out. We pushed it around the office, talked about the cart's specifications, and finally, after thanking the Indesign engineers profusely for this miracle, wheeled it out into the parking lot to load in my car for the drive back to Alabama. I don't remember exactly what Pam and I talked about on that trip, but as we covered those five hundred miles I probably turned my head around five hundred times just to get a glimpse of this beautiful rolling object.

When we arrived home that evening, David met us in the garage to help us unload the cart and we maneuvered it into our dining room. Right away we strapped Caroline in and pushed her around. I have dozens of pictures of that historic moment—Caroline Long, in the cart that not only bears her name but we believe firmly could be her lasting legacy. I stood amazed at God's faithfulness, and I had a glimpse of the difference the cart could make for families across the nation and the world. Standing in our dining room, settling Caroline in for that short ride, we were seeing the unfolding of something that was truly bigger than ourselves.

I was still writing an endless succession of checks, but at long last we had something to show for the expenditures.

At some point that spring, one of the children asked, "Where are we going for vacation this summer?"

David responded, "We're going to go to the dining room and ride around in the cart."

For now, trips out on the pontoon boat and outings to the neighborhood pool would have to be vacation enough. And as exhilarating as it was to finally have possession of the prototype, its daily presence in my house somehow made the other tasks ahead of me weightier. We weren't playing around at creating a product anymore. A cart existed, and it seemed to shout at me to do something that would get it out of my dining room and into some grocery aisles.

My Caroline's Cart team convened soon, knowing that the prototype would trigger some new and vital steps in our endeavor. The most significant milestone that resulted from the meeting was the green light to put Caroline's Cart out on social media. It was something I had been dying to do, but we were in agreement that just talking about the idea wouldn't have a fraction of the power that could be generated by just one photograph of the actual cart.

In April of 2011, I sat down in my kitchen and created the Caroline's Cart Facebook page and published my first post. This was a different type of milestone, but no less significant than finally seeing the prototype. With one photograph of Caroline sitting in the cart in my dining room and a short explanation introducing Caroline's Cart, my crazy idea was unleashed on the nation, or even the world. The beauty and the power of social media is this: You push that "Post" button, and suddenly anyone anywhere has the ability to see that information. Facebook has no borders.

The result was instantaneous and overwhelming. Within hours, people I didn't know were responding to news of the cart with a barrage of questions. "What is that?" "Where do I go to shop with one?" "Is it available for me to purchase?" We only had one cart and no commitment from a manufacturer yet, but through the magic of the internet I had a growing and eager sales force, people I would come to know as "Caroline's Crusaders." It was a bit premature for them to lobby their local stores, but they were out there, ready to pounce on store managers with a vision of what shopping could be for them and their families.

I had used Facebook previously the way my friends used it—to post pictures of my children, connect with old friends, and see what people in my circle were up to. Suddenly I saw it differently—as a vital tool, both to promote the cart and as a source of meaningful encouragement to me as others jumped on board. First hundreds and then thousands of people followed that Facebook page, and I had the best incentive yet to stay the course.

There's an old adage that goes something like this: "In a ham and egg breakfast, the chicken is involved but the pig is committed." As I finally let strangers in on my quest via the internet, it became abundantly clear to me that I was the pig. I was fully in, both because of the money we had already spent and because of the people who were now counting on me to find a way to make the cart available in their local stores.

At the times when I most wanted to throw in the towel, I would find myself thinking of the faces of the families I had encountered through the Facebook page. I would go back and read their words again, drawing energy from the honesty of other parents who had long struggled with grocery shopping and wondered why there wasn't a better way. It wasn't just about me and my family anymore. This was a heavy burden to carry, but also my fuel on the days when all I really wanted to do was curl up next to Caroline and cry.

Another thing that kept me going was the lingering hope that we could forge a partnership with Technibilt. I had left North Carolina the previous year without a commitment from the cart manufacturer, but they had encouraged me to come back when I had a prototype, so that summer my friend Susan and I pulled the seats out of the van again, loaded up my lovely orange prototype, and took it on a show-and-tell trip to Technibilt.

I had a meeting with several of the company's managers, and it was exciting to show them evidence that we were still moving forward with the cart and to share the response we had received via the internet. But even though they were interested and continued to be encouraging, they stopped short of saying they would manufacture it.

For several more weeks I held on to the hope of a Technibilt partnership, until David Orfinik, the vice president for sales and marketing, called to tell me the news I was dreading: Technibilt could not make the cart for us. He didn't go into detail about the reasons for their refusal. I had no intention of quitting, but this was nevertheless a devastating blow. My greatest hopes for the future of Caroline's Cart were dashed.

Nonetheless, we pressed on, and that summer did hold some bright spots. We carefully crafted our first press release for Caroline's Cart and sent it to all the outlets we could think of. As the invisible pathways of social media were transmitting the Caroline's Cart concept to places all over the globe, national media outlets were also starting to take notice. CNN ran a short item on its homepage, and an agency called PR Newswire took a picture of the cart from our press release and did something that kept me up all night because I was so excited—they broadcast a picture of the cart on their jumbotron in Times Square. After the cart had its moment in the Times Square spotlight, PR Newswire sent me a picture of it. Of course I sent it out on my new Facebook page.

The local media was warming up to the story with the help of our press release and a little encouragement from my team. In July of 2011, my hometown newspaper, the *Alabaster Reporter*, ran the first of what would become many print stories about the cart. The article outlined the birth of the Caroline's Cart dream and detailed my progress; it even mentioned that I had made early contact with stores like Publix and Target about offering the cart in their stores.

What is unsaid in print, both in the *Reporter* story and a September article in the larger *Birmingham News*, is the obstacle that was very much on my mind that summer. Despite the successful production and delivery of a prototype and the growing footprint of the cart's message, we still didn't have an agreement with a manufacturer. I was telling newspaper reporters confidently that I believed every store should carry three or four carts. But the truth was, we still only had one—and it was sitting in my dining room.

I love the optimism reflected in this sentence from the *Birmingham News* story: " 'It will also fill a void in the market,' says Long, who is currently seeking manufacturers for the cart and hopes to have them available by the end of the year." That makes me laugh out loud now—it seems to suggest that I had major manufacturers beating down my door and I just had to select the right one. And to have carts available by the end of 2011? The only way we could have had carts ready to distribute in just three months would have been if God Himself decided to create some in our sleep one night and leave them on our front lawn.

I believed He was capable of making Caroline's Cart from nothing, but as months had turned to years I also understood that He wasn't calling me to bring the cart to fruition with any easy shortcuts. The struggle, it seemed, was part of the dream. The price tag of the next phase—as well as the dubious motives of some of the people who would soon enter the picture—would require levels of courage and faith that could have only come from God.

In all your ways acknowledge him,
and he will make straight your paths.

Proverbs 3:6

9

Getting the Word Out

AS OUR SOCIAL MEDIA PRESENCE increased throughout 2011, I started to feel genuine connections with families all over the country who had taken up the Caroline's Cart torch. They certainly kept me going on the days I searched for the motivation to make yet one more phone call, but I was a cheerleader for them as well—responding to messages from countless moms who needed a word of solidarity to help them press on. For some special-needs families who learned about the cart in those early days, the progress of Caroline's Cart became a symbol of hope when caring for a child with special needs felt like a crushing burden.

As I made valuable contacts with allies using the internet, I was also working with my team to plan the first-ever Caroline's Cart video, which featured Caroline and me shopping in the aisles of a Birmingham grocery store called V. Richards. Darlene, from my team, had a connection at V. Richards, which was a small specialty grocery store, and that was a good thing because every other store we tried refused to let us in to shoot the video. We offered to hide the store's identity and to come in at night when they were closed, but no one wanted anything to do with our fledgling promotional efforts. Not one single part of this process was easy, but V. Richards stepped up and helped us out.

That summer brought another surgery for Caroline, one we had long dreaded. Scoliosis is another common complication for Rett girls, and ever since her diagnosis we had steeled ourselves for the news that she would need spinal surgery. When she was diagnosed, we were told that a high percentage of Rett girls would eventually need a spinal fusion, and a small percentage would also need hip surgery. Caroline had both, in two consecutive summers.

That surgery was a major ordeal, and when we scheduled the date for the video shoot we underestimated how long her hospitalization would last. As it turned out, she got out of the hospital on a Friday and then shot the video about a week later—not much time to prepare for her first moment in the video spotlight. It's a wonder you don't see the bags under our eyes when you watch the footage.

The video was a big step because it allowed people to see the cart in action for the very first time. With Caroline riding in the cart, I walked down the aisles at V. Richards shopping and demonstrating features like the five-point harness, the five-degree tilt of the seat for riders with low muscle tone, and the extra space for carrying merchandise underneath. V. Richards was wonderful to work with, accommodating us on a busy Saturday and even welcom-

(Above) The Long family (and Shrek) at Universal Studios in 2016. (Right) Caroline on Easter Sunday, 2010.

(This page, clockwise from top) THE CAROLINE'S CART TEAM Brad Anderson, Darlene Rotch, Dennis Leonard, Randy McClanahan, and Rebel Negley, (Opposite page) The Indesign group working on the first prototype.

03/02/2011

(Above) At Indesign in Indiana, I get to meet the cart for the very first time.
(Below) The guys at Indesign load the cart into my van for the ride to Alabama.

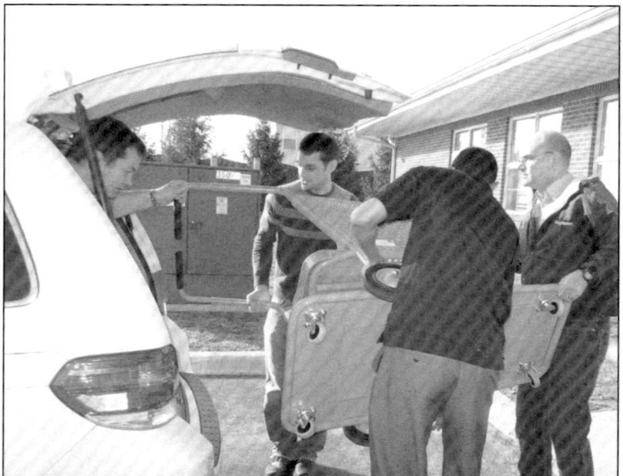

THE CART COMES HOME
(Top) Caroline tries out her cart the night it arrived.
(Middle) David tests out the second prototype. Not every family has multiple shopping carts in their living room.
(Bottom) Matthew and Caroline on our first actual shopping trip with the cart. It works!

(Top) Rebel and me at our first FMI. You can almost smell the fried chicken wings! (Middle) The infamous Budweiser display. (Bottom) Being interviewed for the Washington, D.C., news.

GETTING THE WORD OUT
(Left) With Alabama Governor Robert Bentley.
(Middle) With Florida congressman Ander Crenshaw in DC.
(Bottom) *Good Morning America* tweeted about us!
(Below) I never thought I would see my name in Times Square.

(This page, clockwise from top) Members of Girl Scout Troop 4140 unload the cart in beautiful Alaska. Me with plant manager Alan Deal at Technibilt. Michele Boroughf and her child in Illinois—the very first photo of someone other than my family using the cart! Emma, a happy cart user in California, at Albertsons.
(Opposite page) Amber Delvechio and Alice Little at Technibilt; and the launch invite.

TECHNIBILT®

A wanzl Company

Invites You To Join Us

For the Official Roll Out and Dedication of

Caroline's Cart

Thursday, 18th of July 2013, 11:00 AM

Technibilt, 700 Technibilt Dr

(Formerly East P Street) Newton, NC 28658

Please RSVP by 24 June 2013
Alice Little | 828-468-2507
or at www.carolines-cart.com

Refreshments will be served following the ceremony.

Caroline's Cart™

Celebrate with us as we present the solution to the problem that has frustrated countless parents of special needs children for years.

daVinci Awards 2013 WINNER

Easter Seals Disability Services

(Top) The official Technibilt launch.
(Bottom) Caroline, Rebel, and me with Technibilt executives, including Fred Wanzl and Michael Marks from Germany.

(Top) Charlene Willis and (bottom) Alex Burgess are two of the great folks at Technibilt who make the cart happen.

(Top left) Audrey Rouleau and Stephanie Leclere are two Caroline's Crusaders in Canada. (Top right) Stephanie with her daughter Sarah at Costco in Quebec. (Middle) Me and my Milo's! (Bottom) This photo of Jenny Thomas's 91-year-old mother using the cart was shared millions of times on social media.

(Top left) Addie at a Target in Indiana and (top right) Zachary in Quebec enjoying the cart.
(Middle) My brother-in-law Steve Early with the cart at the military comissary in Huntsville, Alabama.
(Bottom) Darlene Rodrigo and her daughter Bella in a Los Angeles Target.

(Top) Executives from ShopRite and Procter & Gamble join me and Olympic greats Nadia Comaneci and Bart Conner during the ShopRite rollout of Caroline's Cart. (Below) High school student and Caroline's Crusader Haley Smith scores a victory for the cart at her Meijer in Angola, Indiana.

(Top left) Caroline's Cart getting some publicity in Japan and (above) in Honduras.
(Top right) We finally made it to my hometown Walmart, where I had prayed many times for a cart for families like mine.

(Top left) Receiving the National Retail Federation Foundation award. (Top right) One of my favorite family photos—we're getting ready to storm the capitol to lobby for Caroline's Cart! (Bottom) A recent family portrait.

ing us back six months later for a piece on the cart for the Birmingham NBC affiliate.

"She loves to be out, and she's so social, and it just makes me feel so good as her mother to be able to bring her with me where she can participate like a typical child in something just as simple as grocery shopping," I said in the video.

We put the spot on YouTube, where it collected thousands of views in no time, spreading the word to people I wouldn't have reached through Facebook. It also introduced me to the dark side of social media—the stunning cruelty of "trolls" who make it their hobby to hurl angry and unkind missives at anyone unfortunate enough to find themselves in their sights. In response to that first video, a man named Frank commented underneath, "Wouldn't it be easier to drop Caroline off at an orphanage?"

It takes my breath away that someone would be that nasty to any child or mother, and I wish I could say that Frank was the only one. The unfortunate reality of the internet is that when you put yourself out there publicly—even in the name of something so seemingly uncontroversial as a cart for special-needs shoppers—some people will view you as a target. I would be lying if I said the rude comments about my family didn't sting, and often I had to make a concentrated effort to pull myself back into action after reading one of them. But ultimately, those haters faded into the background as thousands of others on Facebook, YouTube, and Twitter affirmed Caroline's

Cart and even went to great effort to lobby their local stores to make the cart available.

Social media has always been my most consistent and effective marketing tool, but I was willing to do anything to help get the word out about the cart. Newspaper and television interviews, plans for more videos, flyers, and the always trusty tactic of grilling grocery store managers were all parts of my guerrilla marketing campaign. But one of my favorite attention-getting tactics—and one I have captured on video in all of its glory—happened in the fall of 2011 on a trip to Washington, D.C.

We had been invited to accompany some Easter Seals representatives to the nation's capital, since Caroline had recently been their National Ambassador, and we attended meetings advocating for the rights of those with special needs, talked with politicians, and tried to tell everyone who would listen about the cart.

One day we were outside the White House gate and we realized that others around us were putting on small demonstrations to further their causes.

We had a stack of Caroline's Cart brochures with us, so spontaneously my mom, Mary Grace, my niece Rachel, and I each held up flyers and started marching in a line and shouting, "Caroline's Cart! Caroline's Cart!" over and over. It was a wonder we didn't get locked up by the Secret Service, but we were absolutely desperate to get a platform for the cart. Anything for the cause! (By the way, the video of that proud moment is still on YouTube for your viewing pleasure.)

Much more professional than our impromptu White House video, our initial promotional video shows me describing the unique features of the Caroline's Cart seat in some detail—like the tilt and the abductor to provide extra support for cart riders. In the real world, though, the specifications of the cart were causing headaches in my dogged pursuit of a manufacturer.

The pressure became especially pronounced, when, in November, I received an e-mail from a Kroger executive asking me for the price and availability of the cart.

Kroger was interested—for all I knew they were ready to order—but we still only had one cart!

I ran into one dead end after another. I learned that there are four companies in the United States in the shopping cart manufacturing business, and since Technibilt had already declined, I started trying to get past the receptionists with the other three.

The managers at Technibilt, in an attempt to keep my quest alive even if they couldn't partner with me, had given me the names of a few other contacts in the industry, including John Ondrasik, the owner of a shopping cart manufacturing company in California. (If that name sounds familiar to music fans, it's because his son John Ondrasik III is the singer/songwriter known as Five For Fighting.) John was taken with my story, but ultimately he didn't think he could make the necessary commitment to my vision. But he was an amazing mentor, offering advice about the industry and even giving me his cell phone number, urging me to reach out if I needed anything.

It was certainly frustrating to face one closed door after another, but I was continually fueled by the kindness and encouragement I drew from the people who were closing those doors. David likes to remind me that "love don't pay the bills," but when smart and business-savvy people believed in me it certainly helped me sit back at that laptop, phone in hand, morning after morning, day in and day out.

Ultimately, each one of the grocery cart manufacturing companies told me the same thing in a different way: They were either unwilling or unable to produce a special-needs grocery cart. Even though I had a team, a company, a prototype, a patent, a much-improved sales pitch, and thousands of families who wanted and needed this product, most retail manufacturers couldn't quite make the leap to produce a cart that had never been seen before.

I did have one offer, via e-mail, from an American manufacturer who assured me he could have carts ready in three months if I would let him take the production process to China. Although tempted, I ultimately couldn't stomach that idea. Years later friends in the industry told me that exporting the cart production would have led to a subpar product and closed doors from major retailers.

The more I learned about the industry, the more convinced I became that the only partner that would really give the cart industry-wide credibility was the one that had said "no" months before—Technibilt.

In early 2012 I made a promising contact with the owner of a fabricating company that created, among other things, the large flat carts used to transport lumber and other materials at home improvement stores. I found him through a man in the business who had heard about the cart on Facebook and called me wanting to help sell it.

I told him I didn't actually have a product to sell yet. Hearing that, he told me about a manufacturer he knew about and gave me their contact information. I called the manufacturer, and after considerable discussion about the cart's specifications he said could make the carts for me, but that he wouldn't be able to produce the seat.

It wasn't a comprehensive "yes," but it was a start, and it energized me to go back to the drawing board in search of a seat manufacturer.

I had learned, from the engineers I had met and others in the industry, that the seat needed to be one piece of high-quality injection-molded plastic. It needed to be comfortable and safe, and to serve the population that needed it the most the seat needed to hold passengers up to two hundred fifty pounds. Many of the families who struggled the most with shopping trips had older children, teenagers, or even adult family members with low muscle tone or other medical conditions that made walking through the store difficult or impossible. The seat needed to work for them.

Like I had done at so many other stages of this pursuit, I called everybody I could find—any company in any city that looked like it might have the capability to produce my seats. I was using words I hardly understood myself, honing my sales pitch all the time as I fished for someone who could produce what was apparently a highly technical piece of plastic.

My learning curve into the world of manufacturing was impossibly steep; I was hearing terms like "injection molding," "structural foam tooling," and "thermoforming," and I felt like I was on Mars. It was sink or swim, and I was paddling like crazy to keep up.

Ironically, the best answer at that time came through Dennis on my team, who had a connection at UAB and knew about a small Birmingham company that was affiliated with the engineering department at UAB. Every other potential seat manufacturer I had spoken with had told me they couldn't do it, so I felt a surge of hope when I contacted the company Dennis recommended and the engineers didn't say "no" immediately. Since their office was so close by, I drove over to meet with them, and that meeting ended with their assurance that they would be able to create the seats for our first one hundred carts.

I knew that the seat was the most important element of the cart, but I never dreamed that the production of that seat would come with such a hefty price tag. My jaw dropped when the Birmingham company told me that it would cost them $80,000 to create the high-quality plastic mold and replicate it a hundred times. Add the placement of the Caroline's Cart and Easter Seals logos, and I was looking at $82,500 for those first hundred seats alone. The cost quoted by the initial cart manufacturer was an additional $36,000—resulting in a six-figure requirement that could have easily stopped us in our tracks permanently.

Our savings account was long since drained, and the unexpected blessing from David's brief period of unemployment had been spent as well—on legal bills, patent applications, and the prototype. If we had any hope of introducing Caroline's Cart to the market, we would need another cash infusion, and Publishers Clearing House had regrettably missed my house so far when they were going around handing out big checks.

One sees great things from the
valley; only small things
from the peak.

G. K. Chesterton

10

A Stake in the Ground

IT WAS TIME FOR ANOTHER serious heart-to-heart with David. It's a good thing God gave the vision for the cart to both of us, because even if I was the one tasked with keeping the train on the tracks, if it derailed the wreckage would affect us all. We were better off if we didn't think about how much money we had already spent—how many college educations it could have funded and how devastated we would feel if it turned out our investment was for nothing.

At this stage, with the prospect of finally producing carts for retail use and a steep price tag standing in the way, we made our most significant decision yet: We agreed to tap into our retirement fund. I can't overemphasize what a faith walk this was. Never in my wildest dreams did I think we would ever have this conversation, and it marked just one of the many times when I was grateful that God had only illuminated small steps of the journey at a time instead of showing me the big picture all at once.

I know it sounds nuts, but drawing money from the retirement account was an easy decision for me. In my mind, we had no choice. I understood that we had put that money away for a season that was still decades away, but somehow at that moment I knew that we needed to use it to keep the cart going. I was the epitome of the pig at that moment—wholly committed, and so far in that turning around wasn't even an option. The only way out of that particular wilderness was to plow through, and the way forward wasn't free. I knew that God had brought us to that point and was still prodding us to continue. He would not abandon us.

But David, as supportive as he was, didn't share my certainty about the decision. He had been raised that you never touch a retirement fund, that you treat it like the Dead Sea Scrolls until you actually reach retirement age.

Initially the idea terrified him. He said, "I remember thinking, we'll get angel investors, we'll get a loan, but I'm not touching this 401(k). But then I felt like God said to me, 'Do you believe it's all Mine? If it's all Mine, then it doesn't matter if it's in a sock or sitting in your 401(k), I've provided it for you.'"

That conviction David felt didn't mean it was easy for him to borrow from that sacred fund—especially when he was the one who had to call the investment advisor and explain that we were going against the advice that was gospel to anyone in his particular profession. David dreaded that telephone conversation, but in the end God used even the scary prospect of bleeding our retirement account as a source of encouragement.

He told the advisor from Fidelity that we had decided to pull a six-figure chunk out of our 401(k), and the advisor questioned him.

"Mr. Long, you do know there are penalties involved if you decide to do this?"

David assured him that we understood the risk and still felt strongly that this was the right course.

So the advisor responded, "Well, can I ask what you need the money for?" I'll let David describe what happened next.

"I thought, 'Oh boy, here it comes.' I squinted my eyes and started to shrink down in my chair and proceeded to give him the short version of Caroline's Cart and the winding road we had traveled so far. I remember there was a pause. And he said, 'That's a fantastic idea.'

"And yet again, I was still waiting for someone along the way to say 'David, red flag, no, no.' Innovation Depot didn't. The lawyer didn't. The Fidelity guy didn't. Everybody was saying, 'This is a great idea.' There were these little pieces of manna from heaven, these little things that said, 'David, you're doing the right thing. Drew, you're doing the right thing.' And that was huge for me."

I had the same experience as David; even when it seemed like I was hearing "no" every hour from someone, no one ever said, "That's a terrible idea. You really shouldn't pursue it." All along the way, I prayed faithfully for God to close doors if we needed to abandon our quest, but even the people who couldn't help us offered consistent encouragement.

The 401(k) decision was an enormous stake in the ground for both of us. It was as if the Lord said, "You thought you had made sacrifices before, but you haven't even scratched the surface. It's time to see how much you really trust My leading in this journey." When we tapped into the retirement fund, we both knew that suddenly this quest was at an entirely different level.

David told me, "Honey, if we're putting our retirement at stake, then buckle up, buttercup. This is your full-time gig. You're going to live it and breathe it."

I already felt that way (remember, I was the pig!) but David wasn't going to let me forget. I had never needed my constant supply of sweet tea and M&M's more than at that moment.

Fueled by those funds and guided by my lawyer and my team, in early 2012 I entered into agreements with both the UAB company and initial manufacturer to manufacture one hundred seats and carts, respectively. Finally, when the growing crowd of people in my social media world asked me how they could use one of the carts, I could tell them that they would actually be available somewhere in the foreseeable future. I knew that a hundred wasn't very many, but it was all we could afford. I was bothered by the sense that we were going to be moving in slow motion unless Technibilt signed on, but it was forward progress nonetheless.

I just knew that 2012 was going to be the breakthrough year for us. The seats would be made first at the Birmingham company and shipped to the manufacturer, and we were hopeful that we would receive carts by summer. It was hard to believe, but soon I could actually go out and take orders, and one day in the not-too-distant future parents would be strapping their kids into Caroline's Carts for dignified shopping trips.

However, as had been the case all along, I would only get to that promised land by way of a grueling uphill climb. It's a good thing I'm an extrovert and believed passionately in the cart, because in early 2012 it seems like all I did was call and e-mail people to plead my case. Even after I had finally solved the manufacturing riddle I needed investors, public relations help, potential buyers, and any kind of free advice that came my way. I was desperate for people with influence to recognize the value in Caroline's Cart and catapult it to prominence so that every step didn't have to be so painstakingly slow. That desperation goes a long way toward explaining the letter I put in the mail in early April.

That winter, through my local Easter Seals chapter, I had met with U.S. Representative Spencer Bachus, an Alabama congressman from my district, and I asked him if he thought I might be able to sit down with President Barack Obama. Yes, I actually asked that question and believed that it could happen. He responded, "I'll tell you what. If you write the president a letter, I will personally put it into his hands." Those are the words he said, but

I can't imagine what this man was thinking. Probably something like, *Who is this lady? How did I end up in this meeting? And what can I say to get her out of here?*

But he didn't know the degree of my stubbornness, so he probably didn't expect me to actually write the president. That letter is so embarrassing to me today, but I'm glad I saved a copy of it because it really does demonstrate the lengths to which I was willing to go to garner national attention for the cart. It's dated April 4, 2012, and it reads in part:

> I would love the opportunity to come to Washington to further discuss Caroline's Cart with you along with other members of Congress and the ADA [Americans with Disabilities Act].
>
> As the saying goes, necessity is the mother of invention. There is no better example of that than Caroline's Cart. From a mom who has worked on this dream from the carpool line, the ball field, the dance studio, and the hospital room, I have a story to tell. Let me tell you more.

Captivating, right? Yet somehow the letter either got intercepted on the way to President Obama's hands or he had more critical things to worry about. That phone call from the White House switchboard never came, but I pressed on.

I was still meeting regularly with my team, and as we strategized we kept coming back to the same obstacle that had dogged me since day one—selling to the retailer. I had galvanized many regular citizens through the Caroline's Cart Facebook posts and other outlets, but since those people wouldn't be the ones writing the checks to buy carts it wasn't enough to have them on my side. I needed some credibility within the retail food industry, and the team concluded to get that credibility I needed to rent a booth at the Food Marketing Institute (FMI) trade show, which was scheduled for late April in Dallas.

I didn't even know what a trade show was before we started the preparations for this trip (I was clueless about every part of this process). Imagine a huge exhibit hall, with one continuous stretch covering 203,000 square feet, holding every food item and accessory that might be of any interest to a professional in the retail food industry.

I came to understand that by establishing a presence at this massive gathering of the players in the corporate grocery world I could gain an audience with the people who could really help the cart take off. Of course, none of the important steps in this journey came cheap, and I soon found out that the very cheapest, smallest booth at the FMI trade show rented for $10,000.

And that was just for the space, my friends! Chairs, tables, lights, decorations—all of those "luxuries" cost extra. I remember asking the FMI people on the phone, "How about oxygen? Is that free?" This was a huge outlay of cash, but despite the steep price tag I knew that the cart needed to have a presence there.

After I reserved my booth, I still had to pay for plane tickets, the hotel, and the astronomical cost of shipping the prototype to Dallas. At the last minute, a member of my team recruited Rebel Negley to accompany me and serve as my on-site public relations specialist. Rebel and I didn't really know each other, even though she had been in the room when I presented my idea to Innovation Depot years before. We had to get acquainted quickly, because Caroline's Cart was on a budget and we were sharing a hotel room. Fortunately, we hit it off right away. I was grateful for her presence because she was a longtime public relations specialist with an extensive sales management background who truly understood how to spread the word about a good idea.

Of course, I wasn't your typical sales representative from a big grocery chain preparing for yet another trade show with networking contacts and expense reports. For me, the days before a trip were consumed with rescheduling Caroline's therapy, buying plenty of food for lunchboxes, and pawning off carpool duty to neighbors. But somehow David and I managed to get it all done so that the Long household would keep trucking and Rebel and I could fly to Dallas to take on corporate America.

Oh, boy. Little did I know how fully invested I would soon be in Rebel's creative marketing schemes. She wasn't shy, and she had an innate knack for salesmanship. We were about to rub elbows with all of the giants in the retail food industry, and my new friend—and future company CEO—was bound and determined to make sure that when those people left FMI they were familiar with a product called Caroline's Cart.

Caroline's Cart

April 4, 2012

Dear President Obama,

Families with special-needs children and adults cannot shop together! It is nearly impossible to push a wheelchair and a shopping cart at the same time. Retailers provide a variety of shopping carts for their more capable customers, but nothing is available for the special-needs community. I am trying to change that.

My daughter, Caroline, is 11-years-old and diagnosed with Rett Syndrome. She cannot walk or talk but is a hero to so many. She is the current National Child Ambassador for Easter Seals and, without speaking a word or taking a step, has the ability to inspire all of those around her...including me.

Four years ago, I started a business to create a shopping cart that would allow me and the millions of other caregivers of special-needs children and adults to shop unencumbered. Caroline's Cart incorporates a seat with a five-point harness into a traditional shopping cart. This allows the disabled to sit comfortably while the caregiver pushes the one unit around the store. Caroline's Cart will allow millions of special-needs families the opportunity to include the **entire family** in the shopping experience.

Suffice it to say, I've learned a lot along this journey. It's not been easy. But I'm happy to say that Caroline's Cart is nearing production and the feedback is better than we imagined! I have received thousands of emails from families all over the world excited to have a shopping option that doesn't include leaving someone at home. From the beginning, that's been the primary objective: for Caroline and others like her to simply be included. For some, it's everything.

All of this brings me to today. Several weeks ago I had requested a meeting with my local Congressman, Spencer Bachus, to introduce him to Caroline and ask for his support. This morning, he honored that request and met with me and Caroline at our local Easter Seals location where Caroline goes for therapy. He was very complimentary and encouraged me to write this letter. I would love the opportunity to come to Washington to further discuss Caroline's Cart with you along with other members of Congress and the ADA.

As the saying goes, necessity is the mother of invention. There is no better example of that than Caroline's Cart. From a mom who has worked on this dream from the car pool line, the ball field, the dance studio and the hospital room, I have a story to tell. Let me tell you more.

Respectfully yours,

Drew Ann Long
Founder and Creator of Caroline's Cart

My actual letter to the president.

For He is looking not for great people but for people who will dare to prove the greatness of their God.

Streams in the Desert

11

Rebel

KNOWN AS THE SUPER BOWL of retail food shows, Food Marketing Institute was a gigantic event, and the placement of the booths was directly related to the amount of money the exhibitor spent on the rent. Picture a football field, where the heart of the action is at or near the fifty-yard line. Then imagine the end zone, and then a remote area *beyond* the end zone, maybe the visiting team locker room. That's where our booth was. We were near the exit door at the extreme far end of the convention center.

We had printed brochures, created a banner for the booth, and of course brought in the prototype so that people could see and push the cart (or, as Rebel said, "kick the tires"), but I felt like country come to town. I was overwhelmed by the number of people and booths, and as we set up our display on the first day I wondered how our tiny presence at the periphery of the action could yield any valuable connections. I felt a little discouraged before we even started, but the next morning there we were, ready to captivate FMI with our groundbreaking grocery cart.

Unfortunately, the only thing that captivated convention-goers for the first day or two was the free fried chicken wings in the booth next door. We were grateful for that chicken display, because the lure of free food was at least bringing people out to the back forty where our booth was located. They fried up those chicken wings from morning 'til night, and when we returned to the hotel each evening, Rebel and I had to shower and change our clothes just to rid ourselves of the chicken smell.

Rebel's role at the show was supposed to primarily be media relations, but she would say that her business mind is more oriented toward sales and managing people and processes, and she felt that we were missing valuable opportunities. We also had two salesmen with us we hoped would help spread the word, but Rebel was frustrated with their efforts and their lack of enthusiasm for the product. (Influenced as she was by chicken smells, Rebel referred to them as our "wingmen.")

After one day of staying in our hidden corner, Rebel convinced me that a different tactic was called for. We walked around more on the second day, trading business cards with anyone who looked at us. Technibilt was there too, with a huge booth near the center of the show, and we stopped by to say hi, to let them know that we were still plugging away.

Our goal was to make every buyer, marketing person, and salesperson in the grocery industry aware of Caroline's Cart. I was excited because I felt like we had so much more traction than the day before, but Rebel was only getting started.

Dead center in the Dallas Convention Center, right on the fifty-yard line, Anheuser-Busch had no doubt paid six figures for the largest and most prominent booth in the place. But it wasn't exactly a booth; somehow they had brought in a Budweiser eighteen-wheeler with a row of beer taps on the side and set it up with free beer samples. Every day in the late afternoon they hosted a happy hour party, and Rebel decided that we were going to crash it.

Rebel said, "I know you're going to think I'm crazy, but most of the buyers are walking the center, and the good thing about what you've got is that it rolls. So sit down and buckle up, buttercup. We're heading down to the Budweiser tent!"

I had already marched up and down in front of the White House and written a letter to the president, so why not ride in a grocery cart and nearly mow down a few happy hour revelers? Evidently making a fool of myself was part of the game, and if I had to sacrifice my dignity for a little more Caroline's Cart exposure, I figured that was all part of proving my commitment to the cause.

She put me in Caroline's Cart, grabbed a fresh supply of brochures and business cards, and pushed me straight through the Budweiser party. Now you need to know that my husband is a deacon at First Baptist Church in Alabaster, Alabama, and deacons' wives most certainly do not crash Budweiser parties. My proper Southern grandmother, who wore white gloves to services every single Sunday, was surely turning over in her grave.

Rebel rolled me around and I did the royal wave all the way through FMI. (Oh, how I wish you could have seen it!)

"I bet I walked seven miles a day pushing that thing for the rest of the show," she laughed later.

The aisles of the show were packed with people, but that didn't stop us. Rebel just kept saying, "Excuse me, excuse me," and we shoved a brochure in the face of anyone unfortunate enough to get in our way.

Rebel was absolutely invaluable to me on that trip. Throughout her career, she has been a successful entrepreneur and also held high-level positions in sales and contract negotiations with companies like Cingular Wireless (now AT&T). She already had a rich list of contacts in the retail food industry and a keen understanding of what it takes to launch a product successfully. She was creative and funny and absolutely relentless in her marketing approach, and she also taught me important lessons—like how to be shrewd about people wanting to take pictures of my precious never-seen-before prototype.

Attendees were not supposed to take pictures at the show, but when someone tried to photograph the cart, I would just smile and let them do it. Rebel knew better and told me to stop letting them do it.

"One of our concerns is people trying to knock off the product," she explained. "They are coming to take pictures because they see it's a great idea and they're trying to copy it."

As we were packing up our no-frills booth when the show closed, we noticed the Tasty Baking Company display across the aisle, loaded down with Tastykake samples. I asked Rebel what they were going to do with all of those little cakes.

She said, "They're probably going to throw them away. Wait just a minute." She marched over there, told the Tastykakes guy that I had three kids back home in Alabama and asked if they needed a home for their samples.

The next thing I knew, we were filling every inch of our Caroline's Cart prototype with Tastykakes. We filled it to the top, shrink-wrapped the whole thing with plastic wrap, and delivered it to the shipping company we had hired to transport the cart back home. It was absolutely hysterical. Rebel and I flew home, and the very next day my doorbell rang. I opened the door and there stood the delivery driver with my cart—full of delicious snacks. That was a delivery my children enjoyed for weeks!

We didn't get a single cart order at FMI, which was okay since we didn't have carts yet anyway, but we felt we had accomplished our mission of raising awareness for Caroline's Cart. Rebel and I might never eat fried chicken wings again, but we served noticed to the industry that the cart was building momentum and that Caroline's Cart would be a player in their game very soon. We came, we paraded around, we conquered, and we got hundreds of free Tastykakes for our efforts.

Rebel's presence at the FMI show made a world of difference, and soon I was relying on her guidance to the point that I started dreaming of hiring her to help me move the company and the cart forward. She was smart and savvy, and she also cared personally about Caroline's Cart and its mission. In fact, in the years between the day she met me at Innovation Depot and the FMI trip, she had seen something at a grocery store that impacted her deeply—a family trying to wedge a larger boy with special needs into a basket whose maximum capacity was thirty pounds.

As Rebel watched the scene unfold, the boy broke his toe, and he was screaming in pain. She made a decision right then that if she had the opportunity to aid our efforts she would do so. "I think the divine inspiration here is that you were not really used to the business world, and I had that kind of experience," she told me later. "And I'm also a mother, and I also knew that you really wanted to do this, not just for Caroline but for the world."

We returned from FMI energized, with our work cut out for us. We had stacks of business cards and intended to follow up with every one of the people we had met. Thanks to the seats being made at the Birmingham company and the carts being produced at the initial manufacturer we could start taking actual orders. Yes, I said orders! The fact that we had actually reached that point in this quest was so huge. The cart had come so close to dying before it had even been born, and now we were chatting with store executives backed by the promise of actual carts.

That spring I made Rebel the first CEO of Parent Solution Group, and she sprang into action. She was an absolute godsend. She made cold calls to grocery store chain buyers (we had learned that every chain typically has one buyer just for carts), pitched my story to trade publications and other media outlets, visited countless grocery stores, and, when the cart hit its inevitable rough patches, joined David in convincing me to stay the course.

One thing that sold me on Rebel was the fact that Rebel Regina Ruth Register (her birth name) knows everybody in the state of Alabama, and I'm not kidding. She decided our first order of business was to visit Governor Robert Bentley. So off to the governor's mansion we went, and we had the opportunity to tell him the story of the cart and take a few pictures with him. It didn't take me long to conclude that Rebel has a flair for the unpredictable.

Hiring her was truly one of the best decisions I made during this season, but there was the issue of paying her salary. We were now two-and-a-half years into this journey, and we still had not seen a single dollar come back to start paying back our retirement fund or our savings. Profit seemed so far out of the question that it was laughable. And now I had added to the ledgers a full-time salary as I continued to write checks for the usual lawyers, patent offices, and manufacturers. Just a year after tapping into the 401(k), our coffers were dry again. And with the size of our debt and no savings, we had learned that we couldn't qualify for a loan.

If this rocky road had taught me anything it was the necessity of persevering. And not just through the many closed doors from people who weren't interested in my product, but also through the fear I felt every time I spent money with no guarantee of return. It was terrifying, and even though I would have cashed out another personal fund if I had one, those sources were exhausted, and I didn't think it would be a good idea to sell our house and live on the streets for the sake of the cart.

I had already been on the hunt for investors, following leads provided by my team, and out of the blue I received an e-mail from a gentleman who lived nearby and was sold on the prospect of Caroline's Cart. He also had the financial means to help us, and we talked about six or eight times that summer before David and I scheduled a pivotal meeting at his house. We were so excited on our way there, thinking that God had led us to this man who could keep our dream afloat.

The meeting started cordially enough, but soon our suitor made it clear that he didn't just want to invest in the cart—he wanted half of our company. In no uncertain terms, he told us that he would only write a check if he could have fifty percent equity, and when we resisted that idea he treated us very unkindly. His demeanor changed completely, and his attitude definitively closed the door on any business relationship we might have pursued. Suddenly this tower we had been constructing, a structure that was finally starting to feel sturdy, felt instead like a house of cards.

In the end, our success is not about us, it's all about God. You take Him out of the equation, you got nothing.

Joel Houston

12

An Angel and a First Lady

THE ENCOUNTER WITH OUR WOULD-BE investor really shook me. After all of our trials, prayers, and risk-taking, this guy wanted to take half of the company away from us? We knew that we couldn't just give it away like that, even if we had to go into further debt to see it through.

When we got back home to Alabaster that night, I burst into tears as I told my friend Jane Gambino what had happened. Jane was a nurse who came to work with Caroline every Friday through Alabama Medicaid. Her wisdom and strong Christian faith made her more like a counselor to me at times, and we had become close friends. She saw more of the inside story than anyone except my family and Rebel. She listened and—more importantly—prayed. Even through the sustained worry about the cart's financing, we all thanked God that we had steered clear of a person whose motives didn't seem to match ours.

There wasn't enough money to move forward, so we kept praying and continued to pursue potential investors. For the umpteenth time, I wondered if this was the end.

When it looked hopeless I had to remind myself that we had often faced places that looked unquestionably like the end of the road, but they turned out to be curves with unexpected detours leading back to the dream.

It wasn't long before God provided an incredible answer to our prayers, and one that was better in every way than anything we had been working on. As it turned out, we had an angel investor in our corner. It was someone I had known for a long time who had the means and the interest in Caroline's Cart to help us out and the generous heart to do so without expecting a financial reward. He had followed our efforts and believed wholeheartedly in our mission. He loaned us $150,000. Needless to say, when he informed us of his decision I was beyond grateful. That loan gave us new life and served as another amazing display of God's provision. (Since this man has always insisted on keeping his involvement in our cause anonymous I will honor his wish. God blessed this man's investment in that ultimately we were able to pay him back in half the time we had agreed upon and he has been thrilled to watch the blessing that Caroline's Cart has been to families around the world.)

For the first time in a long time, we could exhale—secure in the source of the funding that would allow us to keep going. Rebel was a sales whirlwind, making calls to buyers and securing orders that would be filled as soon as the carts were completed. Of course, the presence of Technibilt still loomed large, because when we approached large national chains they all told us the same thing: "We only order carts from Technibilt." We would have to stick to small regional chains and mom-and-pop stores, but those small businesses are in fact the reason for our success. They established a crucial foundation for us as we sought to build demand for the cart.

While we called on potential buyers, we were always looking for opportunities to put the cart in the spotlight, and in July 2012 I saw a television commercial announcing that Michelle Obama was coming to Birmingham on a campaign visit for her husband's re-election bid. Remember, I had already written a letter to her husband, so why not a personal visit to Michelle? But before I could plan my First Lady approach, I needed to be able to get in the door without paying the ticket price (according to the commercial, the tickets were $5,000 a person).

I sprung into action and called my Easter Seals contacts in Birmingham. Did they have a backdoor way to get me into the room with Michelle Obama? It would be huge, I told them, if I could take Caroline and the cart to her appearance. They told me they would do their best, and they contacted the Washington, D.C., Easter Seals office to see if anyone there could pull some strings. Soon I got a call back with the good news—we were in! David had to be out of town that day, but Rebel, my mom, and the kids would accompany me to downtown Birmingham to see if we could get a captive audience with the First Lady.

Security is no joke when the First Lady is involved, so all six of us had to submit our Social Security numbers weeks before the appearance so they could run background checks on us. (I'm proud to say we all passed.) When the day finally came, we piled into two cars (when you travel with a grocery cart you have to sacrifice some seats in the minivan) and drove the twenty-five miles to downtown Birmingham. We arrived, parked in the parking deck near the Birmingham Civic Center, and realized that we couldn't manage both the cart and the wheelchair, so we loaded Caroline up in the cart that bore her name and walked through downtown, an unusual parade indeed.

That building was thick with dignitaries, Secret Service was everywhere, and here we come waltzing in pushing our bright red cart, one of the two prototypes we had received earlier that year from the initial manufacturer (this was in addition to the original from Indesign, so now our house had three shopping carts!). We got plenty of stares when we made our way through security, and at least one official there told us he had never seen a grocery cart come through a security checkpoint. After that we had to split up, because only Caroline and I had passes to enter the meet-and-greet and the rest of them were going to the Obama rally down the hall.

I'm a lifelong Republican just like Granny, but in the other room Matthew, eight years old at the time, thought he was at a rock concert, and was having the time of his life. He was practically plastered in stickers and Obama signs, chanting "Four More Years! Four More Years!" My mother was texting me, hysterical at the mega-Democrat we seem to have produced. While they were getting swept up in the crowd, I was waiting in the meet-and-greet room, and when Michelle Obama came in I waited some more, because Mrs. Obama's people came up to me and helpfully told me that I would have more time with her if I went last.

When it was almost our turn to meet the First Lady, I looked over at Caroline and she was in a deep sleep, slumped over in the cart, exhausted by the ordeal of the day. I woke her up so we wouldn't miss our big moment that so many people had gone out of their way to make happen. We walked around the corner and saw Michelle Obama, who was obviously surprised at what no doubt was the first shopping cart ever pushed to one of her appearances. "Oh my goodness, what is this?" she asked. I was star struck. She was so stunningly tall and beautiful. I could not believe I was standing in front of the First Lady of the United States.

I launched into my fast-talking, word-vomiting mode, telling her about Caroline and the cart, about our story, and trying to fit all of my most compelling sentences into the time I was allotted. I was proud of the cart, but I was also a little humiliated to be standing in front of the First Lady of the land with a shopping cart.

"You know when you go shopping, and you see those fun carts?" I began.

"Dear," she said, "they don't let me go shopping."

Oh, I'm an idiot, I thought to myself.

She told me she thought the cart was amazing and put her hands on my shoulders, saying, "Why is it that every time I hear about a good idea, it comes from a mom?"

Michelle Obama loved the cart, and she even called her chief of staff over and gave me her card, telling me, "I'm going to try to help you. Send an e-mail to my chief of staff and I'll see what I can do."

Of course, I e-mailed her chief of staff thirty or forty times at least, but I never got any response. Nonetheless, it's safe to say Mrs. Obama never experienced a meet-and-greet quite like that one. I like to picture her returning to the White House and telling Barack about the crazy shopping cart lady, and the president responding, "Wait, didn't I get a letter from her?"

I simply won't ever forget that day. I left so full of emotion. I felt ten feet tall and bulletproof. The First Lady of the United States—arguably the most famous woman in the world—thought I had a good idea and encouraged me to keep working on it. It was just the injection of courage I needed. I was convinced that nothing could stop me.

The initial manufacturer thought that the carts would be completed by August, so we were traveling down that road as quickly as regular daily life with three children would allow, finally gathering some momentum, when a call from Technibilt's vice president of sales and marketing stopped me in my tracks.

I had heard very little from Technibilt since the previous summer, when they called to let me know that they would not be able to produce Caroline's Cart. Unbeknownst to me, it turned out, the company had been in an ownership upheaval that had only recently been settled in January of 2012.

Wanzl, a family-owned company based in Germany, bought Technibilt from a private equity group. Now that the initial transition was over, my advocates at the Newton, North Carolina, headquarters felt that conditions were favorable to talk to new Technibilt CEO Michael Marks—who had come from Germany to run the company—about this mom who wouldn't go away. The VP on the other end of that momentous phone call, David Orfinik, recalls what happened next.

"Michael talked to me about all of the different things that were going on in the shopping cart industry, and during our conversations we talked about Caroline's Cart," David said. "And Michael said, 'Tell me more about this.' Then he asked me to talk to Fred Wanzl, our chairman in Germany, and Fred said, 'David, if you really think this is something we should do, let's pursue it.' And that's when I called Drew and I said, 'Hey, what are you doing? How are you doing? Are you making any progress?' "

Michael Marks remembers hearing about my quest to bring the cart to Technibilt and thinking that the introduction of a cart to help customers with special needs was very logical. Bringing in Caroline's Cart was the first decision Wanzl made after acquiring Technibilt, and for Marks it was an easy one.

"My first thought was that the manufacturing of such a product would be a great opportunity for Technibilt to show social responsibility, and I was pretty impressed by Drew's energetic approach to making her idea become reality," he said.

"The decision to produce the cart was taken very fast, as I was convinced that it would be an excellent opportunity for Technibilt and Wanzl to show our customers that we know about their needs and are also willing to do things without looking at profits."

Technibilt wanted us! Without a doubt, this was the biggest breakthrough of our tumultuous journey. Of course, the timing was not great, because I was under contract with the other two companies and awaiting deliveries of the carts they were jointly producing any day. I told David Orfinik that I definitely wanted to go into business with them, but it would have to wait for now. Based on the promise of an agreement, David asked me to get my presentation together and come back to North Carolina to meet with the executives from Germany.

When I visited Technibilt the third time, the mood was entirely different than the previous two visits. Suddenly we were talking more in terms of "when" than "if."

We had two sample carts from the initial production process, and we brought one of those to Technibilt and left it with them.

Rebel, our attorney Randy McClanahan, and I met the new CEO Michael Marks, and we left the building confident that the Technibilt brass was on board. We didn't have a contract yet, but they felt they knew enough to task their engineers to start planning the specifications for their version of Caroline's Cart and the manufacturing considerations that would go into its mass production.

Will Kiser, a product development manager at Technibilt, was given the lion's share of the Caroline's Cart project, and he worked tirelessly to hammer out options that would stay close to my design and keep the cart both safe and affordable. The grocery cart industry is subject to a web of safety regulations governed by the American Society for Testing and Materials (ASTM). A set of standards didn't exist for a special-needs cart like ours because we were breaking new ground. Before they could ever give the green light to make the carts, Technibilt would have to put the design through rigorous safety testing with outside agencies that specialize in quality assurance for retail products.

My prototypes were for plastic carts, and to keep the cart exactly the size and shape of my prototype would require Technibilt to design a custom mold. The amount of labor and sophisticated machinery involved in creating a grocery cart mold, I learned, made it a very expensive proposition. The massive steel mold, which measures around seven feet high and seven feet wide, costs upwards of $175,000 to produce. Suddenly those quotes I heard from other manufacturers along the way didn't seem quite so outrageous.

Technibilt's decision to take on Caroline's Cart was predicated more on the desire to cultivate goodwill than on its potential to make the company a hefty profit, and an expenditure that large didn't make sense before the product was even on the market. Fortunately, they had a plastic cart style that could be adapted with the Caroline's Cart seat, brake, handles, platform, and wheel system.

Late that summer Will came up with a few design options for me to choose from, and they also found a company near the Technibilt headquarters to help design the seat. (Of course, it wasn't lost on me that I had searched for months and months and months to find someone to make this seat, and they secured a deal for their seat with just one phone call. Really? Just one phone call?)

All of a sudden, Rebel and I weren't in this alone; there were professionals at Technibilt, with years of experience in the industry, who shared a stake in my dream and were putting their expertise into making it better. It couldn't happen immediately, but Technibilt's role in the big story we were composing was coming into focus, and it was like the sun came blazing through the thick cover of clouds that had shrouded much of our quest to that point. I had never been more certain that Caroline's Cart had a real, and maybe even profitable, future.

Perseverance is not a long race; it is many short races one after the other.

Walter Elliot

13

Lift Off

WHILE ENGINEERS FINE-TUNED THE NEW, improved Technibilt model of Caroline's Cart in North Carolina, we were still focusing on version 1.0 that was being made jointly by the Birmingham company and the initial manufacturer.

Our most pressing assignment was finding stores to order our first hundred carts (remember, that was quite an investment on our part), and waiting for the day when that first group of carts would finally be ready to ship to those early buyers.

The stores that ordered those early pre-Technibilt carts—stores from seven different states in chains like Belle Foods in Alabama, Hy-Vee in the Midwest, Sunset Foods in Illinois, Price Chopper in New York, and Reasor's in Oklahoma—have a special place in my heart. They didn't have the security of following big chain stores or the credibility of a supplier like Technibilt; they were courageous early adopters acting on their conviction that there indeed was an inequity in the industry and that their customers truly needed Caroline's Cart. There was no red tape—they saw the need and they made a decision to meet it.

Every part of the Caroline's Cart story was important in spurring what came next, and I believe wholeheartedly that our first stores—as well as every dead end we had faced to that point—were vital pieces of the puzzle. Rebel and I were intentional about seeding the market—for instance, trying to get buyers from a diverse geographic area so that those first hundred carts would go as far as possible to spread the word.

Our efforts also served to signal our new friends in the food retail industry that we were serious about seeing the cart progress, even without a big-name partner. Alan Deal and other managers at Technibilt get calls every week from people who have a brilliant idea about something that will make grocery carts safer or more efficient, but most of those would-be inventors have little more than an idea. They want Technibilt to take that idea, lend it their time, capital, and expertise, and make it a reality.

Alan, David, Will, and my other friends at Technibilt have told me they weren't sold merely on the idea I had hatched for a special-needs grocery cart; they were driven to action by the fact that I had poured so much time, energy, and money into that idea. They were courtside as the dream took shape—first as a prototype, then as a rallying point for so many families on social media, and finally as a reality for the stores that placed those early orders—even before they got involved. They watched me struggle, fail, and rise again to each challenge I faced.

Even if it often felt like two steps forward and three steps back, the three-and-a-half years between that first meeting at UAB and Technibilt's involvement represented God's steadfast faithfulness, my commitment to what was at times an impossible goal, and the energy and prayers of the special-needs families who legitimized the need for Caroline's Cart. No one at Technibilt was likely to confuse me with one of those fly-by-night dreamers with a good idea and dollar signs in their eyes.

"All of these who are constantly calling for us to try their latest and greatest invention, their motivation is making money," Alan explained to me. "That wasn't your motivation. You weren't doing this for money; you were being motivated by the cause."

August 2012 was a landmark month because of Technibilt's grand entrance, but we should have been making history for a different reason. According to the timetable we had been given the previous winter, by late summer the first batch of Caroline's Carts should already have been aiding shoppers in stores from Illinois to Alabama, but those carts still had not been produced. To add to the frustration, Rebel and I spent considerable time and money on two separate trips to make presentations to major grocery chains.

First we flew to San Francisco for a meeting with the corporate leadership team for Safeway, and shortly after that we drove to Cincinnati—with the prototype riding in the back of the minivan—to present to Kroger. Rebel and I had a ball on the trips—doing all of the tourist things in

San Francisco and fine-tuning our presentation to make it as polished as possible for the executives in those boardrooms—but the visits weren't immediately fruitful.

Both companies were characteristically complimentary of the idea and supportive of our efforts, but they stopped short of ordering carts, primarily because both companies only ordered carts from Technibilt. Of course, we finally had the seeds of a deal with Technibilt, but it wasn't firmed up enough for Kroger or Safeway to come on board. Those trips served a purpose, though; we were highlighting and advocating for this global, unmet need. A secondary issue, which would soon be addressed by Technibilt, was the fact that they required more rigorous safety certifications than we had undergone.

I wasn't fully plugged in to the bustling activity on the behalf of Caroline's Cart in the Technibilt offices, but I was painfully aware of the silence around Parent Solution Group, where Rebel and I were watching the phone and the e-mail inbox like hawks, awaiting word that our carts were ready to ship. It seemed like that phone call would never come, but in fact God was just looking for an opportunity to remind me, in boldfaced type, that He was still in charge.

The waiting was pure torture. The kids were back in school, our fall routine of dance, homework, therapy, laundry, cooking, cleaning, and carpool had resumed, but I had trouble focusing on anything but the first carts coming out of the factory. By this time, our relationship with the manufacturer had become strained; he wanted a larger order and we were struggling to keep the lines of communication open while holding him as close as we could to his original time frame.

I was grateful for Rebel, because she had decades of business experience and wasn't afraid to lean hard on the manufacturer to keep things moving. She was also out talking, selling, and promoting—pounding the pavement ceaselessly. We exchanged countless e-mails, scheduled too many frustrating phone calls, and prayed morning, noon, and night about what was starting to look like an impasse. Soon it was October, and we still didn't have a delivery date. On the night of October 8, I was cooking dinner and thinking of our plans for Caroline's birthday the next day when I heard an e-mail come in. I glanced down and saw it was from our manufacturer. After all we had gone through, I was nervous to open it.

I mustered my courage and clicked on the message, and I was rewarded with the miraculous news that the first shipment of carts was completed, loaded on trucks, and ready to ship to stores in New York, Vermont, Illinois, Oklahoma, and Alabama the next morning. This was so huge—the carts were shipping! I couldn't believe I was actually hearing that word. The manufacturer said, "I can only send twelve tomorrow, but the rest will be shipped very soon."

He could only send twelve, and the day they would ship, October 9, was Caroline's twelfth birthday! After months of feeling like we were beating our heads against a wall, this was the most vivid sign yet along our journey.

This was no accident; this was God reaching into my daily life to remind me that the cart had been His idea and He was in charge of the timing too. You'd better believe we had quite a birthday celebration the next day.

I think the number of exclamation points in my Facebook post from that day goes a long way to convey what a huge milestone October 9, 2012, was for us. I wrote,

> EXCITING NEWS!! The first shipment of Caroline's Carts are shipping TODAY to 5 states: New York, Vermont, Illinois, Oklahoma, and Alabama.......
> AND, today is Caroline's Birthday!!! This is total coincidence. Bringing a new product to market certainly was challenging. We had been hoping to ship sooner, but we had delays out of our control. This is a sign of good things to come! THANK YOU ALL for your continued support! In honor of Caroline's Birthday, please share this on your wall to help us spread the great news that Caroline's Cart is now in retailers!!! HAPPY BIRTHDAY CAROLINE, YOUR CARTS SHIPPED TODAY!!!!!!!

October 10 brought another significant first. I checked my mail and found an envelope from Sunset Foods, an Illinois chain that had bought a cart for one of its stores. That check was more than just a check; it was a milestone. It wasn't about the money; the check, only for one cart, was a drop in the bucket when you consider how much we owed. But that check legitimized my battle and showed me that I might actually be able to build a business around what had once seemed like a pipe dream.

Money had been flowing in one direction for so long—almost four years—that it seemed almost odd to have someone pay me. Part of me wanted to save the check, but I saved the envelope instead, because we needed that money! I had a retirement fund and a savings fund to replenish, as well as an angel investor to pay back. Making a profit wasn't even on our radar. My remuneration early on came from the precious pictures that began to flood in of kids using the cart. Those happy faces were enough to keep me pressing on.

On October 13, Rebel posted this triumphant announcement on Facebook:

> Dreams do come true—Caroline's Cart officially arrived at Belle Foods in Hoover, Alabaster, and Tuscaloosa!!! Spread the word!

After the initial twelve, another seventy-six carts went out in the next few months to those wonderful early stores that took a chance on us. (The other twelve were destroyed in a fire at the factory.)

I was soon more grateful than ever to have Technibilt waiting in the wings, because during this time Rebel and I handled everything—marketing, sales, shipping, billing, customer service, media relations, and quality control. If there was a question about a brake or a safety concern, the buck stopped with me. But no everyday hassle could contain the joy we felt over this fact: The carts were out there in stores! The families who discovered them were overjoyed, and I treasure the social media messages and e-mails I received from those initial customers.

Some of the press we received from the special-needs community came in the form of complimentary messages praising the cart, but fans of Caroline's Cart engaged in plenty of public shaming of their cities and their specific grocery stores—a very effective form of persuasion that is still being used today. Commonly a special-needs parent or another advocate will ask their grocery store publicly on Facebook or Twitter, "When are you going to get this cart?"

That volunteer sales and marketing force has been the lifeblood of the cart since it made its first appearance on Facebook, and it isn't just individuals who share and like posts about the cart. Many disabilities and medical conditions have private Facebook pages to provide support for people affected by that disorder and their loved ones. Over and over a member of one of those groups would share a tidbit about Caroline's Cart with the other members and they would notify me. Soon I would walk the halls of Congress and meet with the staff of two national disability agencies, but the most powerful mouthpieces I had were actually the other regular moms and dads who had grabbed onto my cause with both hands.

One of the stories that touched me—and also showed me that we still had a long way to go—was that of Haley

Smith, a high school student from Angola, Indiana. Haley was the Hugh O'Brian Youth Leadership representative from her high school in 2012, and as part of the program she was tasked with spearheading a community service project. She chose to raise money to bring the first Caroline's Cart to one of her area grocery stores. I remember talking to her on the phone early in her fundraising campaign, and I recall my response when she told me she planned to donate the cart to a large chain store in her community.

Up until that point, larger chains were still saying no, but we continued hoping to find the angle that would finally break through this seemingly impenetrable wall. Over and over I had conversations with buyers, executives, and store managers, and over and over they said the same thing: "No." Approaching and getting rejected by stores had become a regular part of my Caroline's Cart work, and I had no intention of giving up. But I didn't want this young idealistic teenager to be disappointed, so I warned her that she might want to donate her cart to a different store, preferably one not connected to a big national chain.

But Haley was undeterred, and after a year of hard work, when she had raised enough for one cart she placed her order with me (I covered the shipping costs because I didn't have the heart to mention them to her). I shipped the cart, as she requested, to a store in Angola. The store's assistant manager, to whom Haley had been talking about the cart and who had approved of its delivery, promptly lost his job as a result, and Haley was informed that the cart would have to go somewhere else. Some stores have very specific guidelines dictating the introduction of new equipment to their stores, and Haley's project had circumvented those channels.

The cart ended up in the local Meijer in Angola, where it was embraced enthusiastically by local special-needs families. It would be two more years before we would finally find a way to get the carts into larger chains, but Haley's experience made me all the more determined to keep trying. I'm pleased to say that Meijer would not accept the "free" cart and asked Haley to donate the money she raised to a charity. I was happy to send back the check to her, and we still keep in touch.

In Newton, North Carolina, they were almost ready to produce Caroline's Cart at the nation's largest grocery-cart manufacturing plant, and in early 2013 I would enter into an agreement with them and throw myself fully into this next phase. I would give up a little bit of control as Technibilt made adjustments and recommendations, but I was so confident that they had the power to propel the cart to national prominence that I was willing to step back and join forces with them. The year 2012 had been absolutely groundbreaking for us, but 2013 was dawning with even more promise, with a new partner, and new horizons for the cart.

The size of your dreams must always exceed your current capacity to achieve them. If your dreams do not scare you, they are not big enough.

Ellen Johnson Sirleaf

14

Picking Up Steam

AS REBEL AND I RAN the entire Caroline's Cart operation from my family's kitchen table, those eighty-eight carts did more to create a nationwide movement than anything up to that point. There is no substitute for a mom or dad, long frustrated by their lack of accessibility options at the store, posting a picture of their precious son or daughter in the cart on social media. Naturally, hundreds or even thousands of others in the special-needs community will seize on that small miracle and badger their store managers for a Caroline's Cart of their own.

In early 2013 every new city and state was a singular achievement. We didn't have very many carts, so we still knew where all of them were at that point, and with each new region of the country we raised up a new brigade of Caroline's Crusaders determined to see this new standard available for their children and their neighbors as well. In early February we even shipped a cart to a grocery store in Panama, which was our first inroad into the international market.

We also kicked off the new year with both a new brochure and a new promotional video. We definitely raised the bar with the second video—professional lights, a bigger grocery store as a backdrop, and Caroline wasn't recovering from recent surgery! David and our other two kids even got to appear in this one. The video covered some of the same themes as the earlier spot but emphasized the growth of the cart and the benefits for stores that took a chance on it as early adopters. Those stores would gain customer loyalty from the special-needs families in their community as well as a competitive advantage over stores that weren't offering Caroline's Cart. The video also correctly predicted that the first stores to offer the cart would be the subject of positive media buzz within their community.

Featured in the video was an interview with the manager of the Birmingham Belle Foods that bought one of the very first carts and who had welcomed us to film in his store. The manager's son has cerebral palsy, so his remarks were even more meaningful than those of a grocery store executive who has not experienced the lack of options firsthand.

"These families with special-needs children, they have a place that welcomes them and wants them to come shopping," he said.

There was also a typically optimistic statement from me in the video, based partly on the good publicity we were getting and partly on my boundless enthusiasm for the cart.

"I think it's about to explode!" I exclaimed.

Belle Foods was one store that received a social media boost from the cart, and many others discovered that their local newspapers and television stations did in fact take notice when they became Caroline's Cart pioneers. Local media love a feel-good human-interest story, right? So we saw links from news outlets in places like Lubbock, Texas, Colonie, New York, and others through those early months of 2013, and every word printed or broadcast about the cart helped enlarge our footprint.

Our first group of eighty-eight carts was covering some serious ground, as indicated by the news we received in the first three weeks of the new year alone. On January 17, we received an order from a South Dakota store, and I announced to our Facebook followers that fifteen states now featured the cart. I loved giving "props" to stores like IGA in Cookeville, Tennessee, Fresh Air Galaxy in Hickory, North Carolina, and ACME Fresh Market in Norton, Ohio, that were visionary enough to step out as the first stores in their respective states to purchase a cart. Also that month we received a valuable stamp of approval from one of the top trade publications in the retail food industry.

Writing about the cart and its odyssey in *Supermarket News*, a nationally circulated print and online publication aimed at grocery retailers and others who produce products for retail food stores, Michael Garry explained the cart's purpose and progress and gave us a ringing testimonial. "While I don't normally plug products—whether for-sale or store equipment like this shopping cart—I will make an exception here," he wrote in the publication, which is considered the bible of that industry. "Every store should offer at least one." This was more than a huge testimonial; it gave the cart much-needed validation in the industry.

We were nearing an official agreement with Technibilt at this point, which was both incredibly uplifting because of the potential it represented and a little bit sad because Rebel and I both knew that when Technibilt took over most of the sales and marketing responsibilities she would have worked herself out of a job with Parent Solution Group. But until that contract was finalized, Rebel was her usual whirlwind of activity, spearheading efforts like a meeting with the manager of military commissaries in Fort Lee, Virginia, and a booth at the Tennessee Grocer's Association retail show. She did everything she could to make sure everyone in the industry was aware of the cart. Caroline came along with us on the Tennessee trip, and her presence alone multiplied the interest in the cart. If you ever need to sell anything, Caroline's sweet face is a valuable marketing tool.

In typical fashion, breakthroughs were slow on the military bases, but Rebel's early visits planted a seed that led to big things for families in the U.S. armed forces. In June 2014, about a year after Rebel's first sales call, forty commissaries in twenty-four states had ordered carts, and by the fall of 2016, many Army, Navy, Air Force, and Marine commissaries in the U.S. offered at least one Caroline's Cart.

I also got to share one of the cart's most significant national accomplishments with Rebel that spring, when we received word that Caroline's Cart had been selected as one of three finalists in the Transportation and Mobility category for the 2013 da Vinci Awards. First given in 2001, the da Vinci Awards honor innovation in adaptive and assistive technology, with particular attention given to products that provide opportunities to people with disabilities. We learned in March that the cart was a finalist and that we were invited to the awards banquet in Dearborn, Michigan, in April.

We were excited about that trip, but before the da Vinci Awards we had a pressing engagement in the nation's capital. Rebel and I felt that the cart needed a high-profile boost from policymakers, so we decided to take matters into our own hands in March. Shockingly, President Obama hadn't answered my letter and extended me a White House invitation, but even without an Oval Office appointment we decided to plan a trip to Washington, D.C., with the goal of sharing the Caroline's Cart story with lawmakers and disability-rights groups. This trip had taken months of planning on our part, setting up meetings with politicians and advocacy groups, arranging media coverage, and going to great lengths to make sure our visit had as much impact as possible. Easter Seals was helpful in getting me in front of many of those groups.

Capitol Hill, not Disney World or a beach somewhere, was the Spring Break 2013 destination of the Long family. Mary Grace even brought a friend along. I'm sure our kids would have enjoyed a different place more, but we deputized all of them into our cause, reminding them that this trip was important to the progress of the cart, and Caroline was our secret weapon to gain an audience in D.C. Plus the kids always loved any chance to spend time with Rebel.

I had called my representative and senators and made appointments to visit their offices on Capitol Hill. But when you make those appointments, you don't necessarily see the lawmakers themselves. I saw a lot of people's people. I also did an interview with Alabama Public Radio from D.C. and expressed my hopes for those encounters.

"I would love for the cart to be mandated, just like handicapped parking places are mandated for retailers," I said on the air. "I don't know where it's going to go, but I'm just here to let them know that this is a problem, it exists in every community, and now there is a solution."

With several scheduled appointments to get me in the door of the Capitol building, we just walked up and down the hall, Caroline's Cart brochures in hand, and gave our literature to anyone with an open door.

We spoke with people in the offices of representatives and senators from North Carolina, Florida, and Alabama. We enjoyed an audience with Florida Representative Ander Crenshaw, but in most cases I was talking with congressional aides.

Also on that trip to D.C., we were privileged to be part of the lobbying effort for the ABLE Act, which was written to create new opportunities for people with special-needs all over the nation. ABLE, which stands for Achieving a Better Life Experience, creates tax-advantaged savings accounts for people with disabilities (similar to 529 Plan funds for college tuition), and the money can be used for things like occupational training, housing, and transportation.

All along the way, with the exception of the occasional internet troll, even people who didn't actually offer me any tangible help gave some level of encouragement. Of course, in D.C. we were meeting politicians, so they were adept at saying the things we wanted to hear, but in our purposeful tour of Capitol Hill we ran into quite a few people who told us what a great idea Caroline's Cart was and thanked us for the information.

The trip's objective wasn't merely to schmooze with politicians and their people; we were also targeting the lobbying and advocacy groups that represented the special-needs community. I was given an audience with both the United States Access Board and the National Council on Disability. At the USAB, I gave a presentation to about fifty people, and the meeting at NCD was a smaller roundtable discussion. Rebel and I were in full advocacy mode. It certainly made for a memorable birthday celebration for her, as she was marking her Big 5-0 on the trip.

What was I hoping these groups could do for me? I truly didn't know. I didn't even know exactly what their reach or their policy-making ability was, but I knew we cared about the same issues and that they had more power and connections than I did. If they could do anything at all to help the cart along, I figured it was worth me asking. It was nice to get a seat in the room and have people in the special-needs community listen to me.

Media attention on the cart was continuing sporadically during this time, but while we were in D.C. I was asked to do an interview with the Washington ABC affiliate thanks to a Birmingham friend who was the general manager of our local ABC station. It's hard to measure the footprint of a regional interview or newspaper story, but I like to think that every time the Caroline's Cart story is broadcast to a new audience new Caroline's Crusaders are born—people who either need the cart themselves or believe so strongly in the need that they become a persistent presence in the life of their local store manager.

This was an amazing trip, and although I still didn't get my meeting with Mr. Obama, our mission was complete. Every person we met said, "Why has this not been done before?" The drive home seemed to fly by, because I was so energized by the encouragement I had received from my new friends in the nation's capital.

With our lobbying adventure behind us, Rebel and I looked forward to the April da Vinci Awards, and in the meantime we lobbied our Facebook supporters to vote for Caroline's Cart in the separate da Vinci social media contest. A different product won for most "likes" of their video, but we won for the Mobility and Transportation category. The people associated with the da Vinci program see a lot of products and truly understand the landscape of adaptive technology, so this was another validating experience.

While Rebel and I jet-setted—from California in late 2012 to Washington, D.C., and Michigan in early 2013—the Technibilt headquarters were abuzz with their own Caroline's Cart tasks. That February, Will Kiser spearheaded the process of putting their sample cart through the rigorous product testing by an agency called Bureau Veritas. About a month later, Technibilt received a fifteen-page evaluation requesting some minor changes to the design to ensure optimal safety—adjustments like adding a UV inhibitor and corrosion protection to the seat (those features already existed on the basket), and increasing the durability of the straps.

Finally, later that spring, Technibilt let us know that the cart met their exacting specifications. Now we were ready to set a schedule for the first official production run. But first, we had to reach the terms of our contract—an agreement that would retain my voice in the development, growth, and marketing of Caroline's Cart, while handing the details associated with sales, production, and distribution to Technibilt.

As we defined the terms of our partnership—culminating in the signing of our official contract late that spring—it became clear that the day-to-day management of Caroline's Cart at Technibilt would fall to Alice Little. Alice, who had come to Technibilt from the furniture industry in 2007, handled other sales and marketing responsibilities before we signed our contract, but starting in the spring of 2013 she became the chief customer service and marketing representative for Caroline's Cart.

As Alice will tell you, she loves her job. I kept the responsibility for maintaining the Caroline's Cart social media accounts, but she took on all of the telephone and e-mail inquiries and testimonials about the cart. Every day she hears from people who love the cart, and every day she guides those who are still campaigning for the cart by walking them through the process of printing off brochures and "Dear Manager" letters from the Caroline's Cart website. She would become the cart's number one advocate and one of my dearest friends, but as the summer of 2013 approached, her most pressing task was planning a big public launch for Caroline's Cart at Technibilt.

Everything is impossible
until it is done.

Robert H. Goddard

15

Technibilt

THE TECHNIBILT LAUNCH WOULD BE a big event—the invitation list included elected officials and dignitaries from the region in North Carolina where the company was located, the media, special-needs families, and grocery store managers—and members of the Wanzl family would fly in from Germany for the occasion. But as July 18 approached, we wondered whether the guest of honor would even make it.

Ten days earlier, Caroline had been hospitalized with seizures, and she was still on the ventilator just days before we were scheduled to leave for North Carolina. The day before, with Caroline still in the hospital, we created a contingency plan in case she wasn't able to make it. David would stay back in Alabaster with her and I would travel to Technibilt with the other two kids. It was stressful, because we really wanted Caroline and David to be there, but she was very slow to stabilize.

Miraculously, spurred by the prayers of many, Caroline rallied, and we were able to make the six-plus hour drive as a full family of five. We arrived in North Carolina and fell into our beds in the hotel, exhausted from the ordeal of the past days but exhilarated by the prospect of what the next day would hold. The launch was scheduled for eleven a.m. at the Technibilt headquarters.

After so many years of desperately seeking legitimacy—from retailers, manufacturers, engineers, and any other entrepreneur or expert who crossed my path—that day was the ultimate validation. Not only had Technibilt recognized the value of Caroline's Cart and put their time, money, and resources into bringing it under their roof, they were holding a celebration for the cart—an event so significant that executives traveled from Germany to be there. Most of my original team were able to be there as well—Darlene Rotch, Randy McClanahan, Brad Anderson, and of course the irrepressible Rebel. It was such an exciting time for us, to literally see our dream come to fruition in the most concrete way.

Alice Little and the others who had planned the launch thought of everything; every detail was just perfect. They decorated the sample cart with huge yellow bows and Alice had even customized the cupcakes with Caroline's Cart decorations on each one.

I had been asked to give a speech, and it was absolutely surreal to be there, speaking about the dream that had seemed so impossible not so long before, to a group of people who sat at the center of the grocery cart industry. It was heady stuff, but if I had to remind myself that I was still an ordinary mom from Alabaster I only had to reach back twenty-four hours, when I had been holed up in a hospital room with Caroline. I stood in awe of our journey to that point—the hurdles, the struggles, the failures—and I could not believe we had actually made it to the launch.

After David Orfinik from Technibilt gave a presentation about the history of the cart, CEO Michael Marks introduced me. After my speech they presented a Caroline's Cart to Caroline and then David came back up and gave a wrap-up speech. After the presentations, we had refreshments and tours of the Technibilt production facility. Everyone from Technibilt talked about how happy they were to have the cart, how necessary this product was for so many families. It was a day my family and I will never forget.

In a press release disseminated to media outlets two days before the launch, David Orfinik said,

> Technibilt is thrilled to be a part of this amazing grocery cart for children with disabilities. It is going to provide families the opportunity to shop with their child with a disability, with the same ease as a typical child. We thank Caroline's mother and inventor of Caroline's Cart, Drew Ann Long, for recognizing this need and having the strength and fortitude to make it come to fruition. We feel that retailers and grocers worldwide will embrace this opportunity with open arms.

Those were encouraging words, and if the amount of effort they put into the launch was any indication, Technibilt had certainly jumped into the cause of the cart with both feet. Suddenly, I wasn't the only pig on the Caroline's Cart farm. The truth was, at that point they had taken a huge gamble. They didn't know whether Caroline's Cart would be profitable for them at all, and some there even framed their involvement with the cart as a way to be a good community partner regardless of its financial potential.

The cart would eventually surprise everyone with its earnings, but that day on the podium, with the cart that I had once sketched on a napkin sitting beside me, I still knew very little about what lay ahead. More doors would slam shut, but at least now I wasn't facing those rejections alone. I had the weight of an influential company behind me, and just as I had always believed Technibilt held the key to the cart's success, I was confident that this celebration was the jumping-off point for something big.

July 18, 2013, was a banner day, and we returned to Alabama with our spirits soaring. But even though Technibilt and I had united and enjoyed a honeymoon period, I struggled later that summer with the reality that I had relinquished control of the thing that had driven me for years. Technibilt still wanted me to be the face of the cart, which would allow me to attend trade shows and other events and participate in marketing videos and other promotional pieces. In those early days, selling the cart was like settling in the Wild West—we didn't really know what we were doing, but it was exciting and every victory was huge.

Suddenly, sales were out of our hands, and as of that summer Rebel was a former employee of Parent Solution Group. She still says that she happily worked herself out of a job—that she had hoped all along to help link the cart with a big, national company that could give it the funding and marketing it deserved. "It made me happy to know that I was a part of it, that I helped to make a difference," she said. Without a doubt, she was a gift from God. When I thought I might perish in the desert of rejection and discouragement, Rebel came along and brought the refreshment of her expertise, her persistence, her encouragement and her uncanny ability to make me laugh. I missed her desperately, and as soon as she was gone I started trying to find a way to bring her back. Rebel always referred to herself as my handler, and with her gone who would supply my steady stream of sweet tea and M&M's?

Rebel moved on to an interim CEO position with another Alabama firm, but I felt adrift. A partnership with Technibilt had been the Holy Grail for me, but now that my huge quest was over I didn't quite know how to behave. It was an abrupt halt. I was like a mother who had birthed a baby and taken care of that baby for four-and-a-half years and then given that child up for adoption. Caroline's Cart would always be my baby, and everyone at Technibilt was absolutely respectful of that fact, but someone else had taken over as the guardian. Alice was my lifeline, staying in touch daily about the e-mail inquiries she received, the progress of the cart, and the status of orders. I was a little lost, but not for long, because the pace of life with three kids was getting busier than ever.

Sales started off slow but steady, but sales are sales, and I was thankful. The big retailers had been asking for Technibilt, and we had finally delivered! I guess I expected a huge avalanche of orders to come in the minute Technibilt put its name on the cart, but I still had a thing or two learn about the corporate world.

Spurred by the continued pressure being applied by the special-needs community on social media and the credibility of the Technibilt name, the sales numbers did climb that fall and winter. But I began to realize that the style of salesmanship with Technibilt taking the lead was quite different from the approach Rebel and I had been taking as the Caroline's Cart Dynamic Duo.

Technibilt has been in the grocery cart business since 1946—starting in California before moving to North Carolina—and with those decades in the industry come trusted relationships with some of the top food retail companies. They supply typical grocery carts to Walmart, Kroger, Home Depot, and Publix, to name a few. So when they added Caroline's Cart to their offerings and started pitching it to their longtime customers, they weren't about to push as hard as I would. I was, after all, a renegade special-needs mom with one product, nothing to lose, and a tendency to get overexcited.

Typically when I got an audience with a store manager, I would start by giving a rundown of the various carts

I saw in their store—carts that would serve a variety of populations. Then I would tell my story, introduce my cart, and inquire as to why every other person who needs shopping assistance gets a special cart when kids like Caroline are ignored. Over time I learned that you catch more flies with honey than vinegar and gentle encouragement seemed to be the best way to go. This product was entirely new to the industry, and some stores just needed more time than others to marinate on the decision.

Technibilt's sales team couldn't exactly use my guerrilla tactics, because they couldn't risk sabotaging their long-cultivated connections. I don't blame them for not wanting me in the room during sales meetings; the managers there have spent enough time with me to know I'm a bit of a loose cannon when I get passionate about the cart. I remember e-mailing David Orfinik to let him know I was a willing salesperson, writing, "Send me in, Coach!" But I knew, and the Technibilt folks knew, that I'm kind of a bull in a china shop sometimes.

Of course, that didn't stop the army of cart supporters out there from calling out their local stores who refused Caroline's Cart or starting online petitions for either individual stores or chains to pay attention to the shoppers who had been lobbying for it. I never encouraged this activity, but I sure understood and felt their frustration. And as Alice became the voice of Caroline's Cart at Technibilt and started to field e-mails and phone calls, I turned more of my attention to the people I had met who were pouring their heart and soul into the cause of the cart.

Every day I had the opportunity to encourage people who reached out to me on the internet or to Alice through e-mail, even if there truly weren't enough hours in the day to answer every message. I became acquainted with Crusaders like Allison Foley, a doctor in Orange County, California, who had grown weary of the struggle of grocery shopping with her daughter Emma who, like Caroline, has Rett Syndrome. Allison learned about the cart through a Rett's page on Facebook and went to work advocating in her community.

She lobbied her local store, facing multiple refusals—even when she offered to buy a cart herself and donate it. Finally, late in 2013, her local store notified her that a Caroline's Cart had been ordered and would be available by Thanksgiving. "I call it princess shopping," Foley told *The Orange County Register*, which ran a feature about the cart that December. "It's just like a dream."

Amid the flurry of good reports from all over the nation (we were even featured on an ABC broadcast in Montana), we continued to reach milestones in the retail industry as orders came in from new stores—ShopRite in August, new locations of Kroger and Publix in October, Whole Foods in November, Albertsons, and Hannaford in December. We weren't taking over the world yet, but every week, it seemed, more special-needs families were simplifying their shopping outings with Caroline's Cart. And the Crusaders didn't have just grocery stores in their sights; people were also lobbying home improvement stores, hobby stores, and discount warehouses.

My office could still be found wherever I was—my kitchen table, the carpool line, the dance studio, the doctor's office, the hospital—and my life as a mom was as busy as ever as my children grew older and took on new activities and more difficult academic challenges. With Technibilt helping drive the train, I was settling into my new role and enjoying the view as I watched the dream that I had carried for so long grow in scope and make a difference for thousands of families like mine.

Sometimes when you believe the impossible, the incredible comes true.

Field of Dreams

16

Crusaders in Action

IF I NEEDED EVIDENCE THAT I was finally part of a larger and more influential team in my efforts to grow Caroline's Cart, I needed to look no further than the trip I took in February of 2014. I had to make sure my passport was up to date, because I was to be part of the Technibilt contingency at EuroShop 2014 in Düsseldorf, Germany. It was only five days, but the prospect of my departure for Europe led us to schedule a procedure for Caroline to have a feeding tube put in. She didn't eat well for David, and he was afraid that she would become dehydrated by the time I returned to the States.

Rebel was no longer officially employed with my company, but her presence had been so crucial in the cart's growth to that point that she was invited to come along. There was no way I could go without her. We had come a long way from our booth in the corner near the fried chicken wings at our first trade show! EuroShop is absolutely massive—almost thirty acres of floor space housing over two thousand exhibitors from sixty countries.

Because Wanzl was a large company based in the show's host nation, our backdrop was an elaborate, sprawling booth featuring, among other Wanzl merchandise, a shiny Caroline's Cart. Actually, it's a misnomer to call Wanzl's display a booth; their setup was literally larger than my house. It had two floors, full kitchens upstairs and downstairs, a coffee bar, seating for over a hundred people, and servers delivering food and beverages to visitors. It was a palace!

EuroShop was an amazing experience for us, even if we didn't speak the same language as most of the people who stopped by the booth. Visitors from countries as far away as Egypt and Australia showed significant interest in the cart—and Rebel and I didn't even have to parade past the Budweiser exhibit during happy hour. Not only did the show serve as an international public relations win, it cemented my relationship with the executives from Wanzl and Technibilt who were helping me carry the future of my product. I was now on the team; maybe just the waterboy, but I had a role. I even got to talk with Mr. and Mrs. Wanzl at the show, and they were gracious and appreciative of their company's relationship with the cart.

Through the first half of the year, the orders coming into Technibilt ticked upward every month, and in May came word of a huge milestone—the first comprehensive rollout for Caroline's Cart. Until that point, all of our orders had been piecemeal—a Kroger store in Georgia, a Publix in Florida, a Food Lion in North Carolina. It was a big event when a chain purchased carts for more than one of its locations in the same city at the same time.

But then in May, two companies dreamed bigger—embracing Caroline's Cart as part of their corporate identity. That May, first Wegman's, a New York-based chain, and then ShopRite, a New Jersey-based chain with stores in six Northeastern states, decided to purchase carts for every one of their locations. Those decisions meant that by summer of 2014 more than three hundred new stores would be offering carts to their customers!

The willingness of those two companies to be pioneers by making Caroline's Cart standard equipment was a huge boost for us. If ShopRite and Wegman's could do it, then why not Kroger, Target, or Walmart? Adding to our excitement was the invitation our family received to a special celebration of the ShopRite rollout in late May. The ShopRite carts were provided to the stores through a partnership with the consumer goods giant Procter and Gamble, as a promotion of their sponsorship of the Special Olympics. P&G's involvement was incredibly gratifying for us—they were a huge national brand, and they even put their logo on all of the ShopRite carts.

Because of Procter and Gamble's relationship with the Special Olympics, and because the Special Olympics also served the special-needs community, the ShopRite deal connected us to them. This was exciting because, like Easter Seals, Special Olympics has done a great deal to raise awareness about children and adults with special needs. (I'm proud to say that Caroline has been a participant at the local level for years.) The collaboration also allowed me to meet a couple of my childhood Olympic heroes. With eleven Olympic medals between them, Nadia Comeneci and Bart Conner must be the world's most decorated married couple, and they also serve on the board of directors for the Special Olympics.

It was a memorable Big Apple vacation for our family—we saw Broadway musicals, visited the bakery featured in the show *Cake Boss*, and even learned how to navigate the New York subway system with a wheelchair.

After soaking up the sights of the city for a couple of days, we traveled across the river for the Caroline's Cart unveiling, which featured a ton of media coverage, Bart pushing Nadia around in the cart, and lots of food. We even went home with copies of the ShopRite weekly chain-wide circular with a splashy advertisement for Caroline's Cart inside. The ShopRite executives told us that the circular went to nine million mailboxes! It was, up until that point, the biggest thing that had happened in the life of the cart, with the possible exception of meeting Michelle Obama.

Those trips to Germany and New York were both encouraging and beneficial to our goals for the cart, but they did present one problem. When I went on the road for several days I would return to a crushing flood of e-mails and social media messages. I thought Caroline's Cart was taking over the internet in the years between the prototype and the Technibilt deal, but I hadn't seen the half of it.

For most of 2014, I'm convinced I could have sat in front of my laptop twenty-four hours a day, seven days a week, and still not managed to respond to every message. I heard from parents worldwide who had seen a post about the cart and wanted to know how to start the ball rolling at their grocery store, from community activists who wanted to raise awareness or raise money for a cart in their town, and from those who had been lobbying store managers for weeks, months, or years to no avail.

I felt the most responsibility for that last group, because I understood the rejection they were facing. I knew firsthand what it was like to hear the reasons why a Caroline's Cart would never work in their store. "We don't have special-needs families in our community." That was always my favorite. My response (with a smile on my face) was, "Yes you do. Your store is just not accessible, therefore you don't see us. That's why we call ourselves the invisible population."

I have heard the word "no" so often, and with so many excuses attached, that I'm numb to it. I like to prepare the Caroline's Crusaders: Managers will tell you their customers don't need it, that they can't afford it, that they don't know if "corporate" will allow them to order it. More and more, as we have gained a foothold in the industry, those excuses are invalid, but the store managers don't always know that. Eventually we wrote a "Dear Store Manager" letter and uploaded it to the Caroline's Cart website so that Crusaders could have the cart brochure and the letter quick at hand when they faced resistance from local stores, which was happening far too often.

As much as I saw myself as a cheerleader trying to keep people going when they felt like a punching bag, I also read several stories a week that made my heart soar. All over the nation, in cities I had never heard of, ordinary moms and dads just like me were fighting for the cart; and for every intransigent store manager who refuses to budge there is one who puts the wheels into motion to get a cart in his or her store.

Alice and I have received so many beautiful pictures of children and their parents shopping with the cart—so many mile-wide smiles from the kids who are comfortable, safe, and included—that Technibilt eventually used the images to create a video that they unveiled at the company's annual sales meeting in 2016. When the video was over, we had to pass the tissues!

We also saw the power of social media on display over and over, and my learning curve was steep as I explored the potential of newer platforms like Twitter and Instagram. One of my favorite stories came from a dad named Doug in Kentucky.

Initially, Doug had a tough time even setting up a meeting with the store manager at one of his local stores. He was put off time and again when he tried to be heard in his efforts to get a Caroline's Cart to make shopping easier with his daughter. One day he was on Twitter, and he noticed that the person who managed the company's Twitter account was replying to customers' tweets. Seizing the opportunity, he tweeted to the store,

> Hey ... how do we get @carolinescart in your stores? Manager won't call us back about it. What's the deal?

This commenced a conversation on Twitter between Doug and the retailer's representative, who promised to find an answer. The next day Doug's phone rang, and the manager of his store was on the other end. Just a couple of days later, the store had placed an order for a Caroline's Cart. It just goes to show that in this digital age, 140 characters can be far more powerful than any petition.

As the steady flow of messages became a tidal wave, I was more grateful than ever to have Alice in my corner. She received many of the messages sent through the Caroline's Cart website and those that went directly to Technibilt, and she was able to respond to a large percentage of them herself. But when something required a personal bit of encouragement, or when a message included a story she knew I would want to read, or when she just didn't know how to respond, she would send it on to me.

And our product wasn't just a darling of cutting-edge social media. Over and over, in small regional markets and on a national scale, the news media deemed the Caroline's

Cart story worthy of airtime or column space. Every time I worried that our story was losing steam, someone would send me a link to another story, usually because a local Caroline's Crusader had finally won the battle and alerted the media. Every one of those mentions served as evidence to us that God was in charge of this cause, and He had no intention of letting it die down.

One of the most exciting articles, in terms of its scope, was a March 2014 feature in *USA Today*. The main feature on the newspaper's "State-By-State" page told the story of a Wisconsin mom named Sandy who e-mailed a regional grocery chain called Festival Foods explaining the challenges of shopping with her son, who has cerebral palsy, and asking them to order a Caroline's Cart. "If you see something out there that could help another family, don't be afraid to ask—the worst they can say is no," she told *USA Today*'s Nick Penzenstadler.

Festival Foods had nineteen stores at the time, and after Sandy e-mailed about one location and another customer requested the cart at another, they made a corporate decision to offer a cart in every store. Just two requests, and in no time, nineteen grocery stores became accommodating and safe for special-needs families. How I wish it were always that easy!

When a tweet or an e-mail alone wasn't enough, we heard stories of persuasive customers employing a number of tactics to spur their favorite store to action. Take the case of a mother of a Rett Syndrome daughter in Portland,

Oregon, who contacted me for guidance about getting a cart in her local location of a national chain. I tried to prepare her that a protracted battle might be ahead, and she said, "No, this is going to be really easy. I'm just going to talk with the store manager and tell him that if he doesn't order Caroline's Cart I will call my local Fox TV station's On Your Side reporter, who will come stand in the parking lot and interview him about why he won't help my daughter." She did exactly that, and before she knew it her store was ordering Caroline's Cart. The TV news reporter never even had to be called.

The first daunting obstacle, for any Caroline's Crusader, is just getting in front of the store manager. Often they don't want to field complaints or suggestions, claiming they are too busy and leaving customer interactions to other employees. But the store manager is the linchpin for our efforts; he or she is the one who generally has to place the order for the cart. When a store manager finally takes the time to listen and respond, the next step is often a call to Alice at Technibilt.

"They call me and say, 'I don't know about this cart,' " Alice says. "And I tell them, 'Your corporate office has already approved it, it's in your system, and here's your cart number so you can order one.' "

Those calls were becoming more and more frequent for Alice in the summer of 2014, and I finally felt like the cart—a dream that had almost become a permanent nightmare before Technibilt came on board—was gaining a foothold in such a variety of regions and grocery chains that it could finally be categorized as a new standard. We were still hopeful that Walmart, Target, Home Depot, Lowe's, and others would say yes, but all we could do was press on with gratitude for the miracles God had worked already, and faith that He wasn't done with us—or the cart—just yet.

The LORD will fight for you,
and you have only to be silent.

Exodus 14:14

17

Hitting the Bull's-Eye

IN THE SUMMER OF 2014 I got to return to the event that Rebel and I had experienced from the far end zone two years earlier—Food Marketing Institute, or FMI. Like EuroShop, the June show in Chicago was an entirely different experience under the umbrella of Technibilt. I was part of their team, and we had a big, fancy booth in the middle of the convention floor, near the fifty-yard line. No more smelling like fried chicken wings for me!

Any time I experienced the grocery industry with the Technibilt team as my tour guides I learned more, and in some ways my expanded understanding made the cart's progress even more miraculous than I had ever understood it to be. In the years before Technibilt, one of my best assets had been my cluelessness, my belief that a mom truly could develop a shopping cart, have it produced, and sell it to retail stores.

If I had known, back in 2009, how expensive it is just to produce a mold for a custom cart, how nearly impossible it is to even have a conversation with the grocery cart buyer of a large chain, how unyielding every aspect of the retail food world can be, I believe I would have thrown my drawing in the trash can, held Caroline close, cried, and then moved on to a house improvement project or rearranging my spice cabinet—anything but create a new kind of grocery cart.

But you don't know what you don't know, and by the time my eyes were opened I was safely ensconced in Technibilt—feeling responsible for keeping the Crusaders energized, but relieved by the number of details that were no longer under my purview. I had a different role now, and I took it very seriously.

I was as busy as ever—taking care of Caroline and managing Mary Grace and Matthew's schedules was never less than a full-time job—and the everyday stresses were amplified exponentially in July when Mary Grace had to have back surgery (essentially the same surgery for scoliosis that Caroline had undergone three years earlier). This was ten times harder than one of Caroline's hospitalizations, which were such a regular part of her life—this was one of my healthy children, a young lady who danced for hours a day, and I was unaccustomed to worrying about her health or seeing her incapacitated. Like I had before, I took my laptop and worked on every aspect of the cart mission from the hospital, taking inspiration from stories like the one that reached us all the way from Sitka, Alaska.

At that point Alaska didn't even have a single Caroline's Cart, but several members of Girl Scout Troop 4140 heard about the product and took it upon themselves to bring the carts to their town of nine thousand. Through a series of fundraisers, the scouts raised more than $2,000—enough to order a Caroline's Cart for each of Sitka's three grocery stores. They kept in touch with Alice and me, sending us pictures of the cart deliveries and links to the news articles that highlighted their accomplishment. Because they started the Alaska ball rolling, carts continue to be ordered by new stores there today—a movement made possible by a single rural Girl Scout troop!

As much as I draw encouragement from stories like that and feel a strong connection with the people whose determination brings carts to even remote places, I am a little bit puzzled by them too. Did a non-profit organization or a group of service-oriented teenagers have to raise money so that their local grocery store would carry an electric scooter or fun cart? I've never heard of a campaign like that, even though the scooters cost more and most stores carry three or four. When fans of the cart started attaching #newstandard to posts about it several years ago, the implication was clear: Caroline's Cart should be required equipment for grocery stores, lined up with the toddler carts and the fun carts and electric scooters before a new grocery store even holds its Grand Opening.

I can't wait for the day when the cart is so common in retail settings that no one needs to hold car washes and man lemonade stands just so that their neighbors with a special-needs child can enjoy a shopping trip. As more and more chains approved the cart and put it into their internal systems, Alice encouraged people who called her to engage in a different kind of service project, one devoted solely to public relations.

When a retail chain is in the system, Girl Scouts and Rotary Clubs and high school students seeking service hours can skip the fundraisers and instead print brochures and "Dear Store Manager" letters from the website and make a plan to blanket their community with a Caroline's Cart awareness campaign. Our experience is that when managers understand the need they're happy to order a cart. My hope and prayer is that eventually even that type of marketing blitz won't be necessary, but for now it is an excellent way to keep the cart front and center until every store everywhere is equipped with at least one. With over thirty-seven thousand grocery stores in America alone (not to mention thousands more non-food retailers), we have a ways to go!

Slowly but surely, throughout 2014, we were putting more pins in the map. And the cart was even starting to gain a foothold overseas—in 2014 alone we sold Caroline's Carts to stores in New Zealand and Alberta, Canada, and we heard about a campaign to raise awareness about the cart in, of all places, Turkey. We even received some orders from Walmart stores in Canada, marking the first time a Walmart had featured the cart. And the touching stories kept coming in—like the one about Carolina Alfaro from Turlock, California, who was profiled in August 2014 in *The Modesto Bee*.

Two of Carolina's three sons, Diego and Adrian, had a rare genetic disease called Zellweger Syndrome, and tragically neither lived past his third birthday. Carolina didn't read about Caroline's Cart until after Diego and Adrian had passed away, but it brought back the days when she would try to shop with one of her boys and the frustration those trips to the store would bring. Before long, this hero—who could have just wallowed in her own loss—was calling every grocery store in her region and asking managers if they had heard about Caroline's Cart. Her lobbying efforts paid off, and soon three nearby stores ordered carts—two at Save Mart locations and one at a Trader Joe's. Eventually, due to her advocacy, every Save Mart store in California ordered a cart.

I felt I *knew* women like Carolina. We shared so many of the same struggles as well as a passion for the cart and the doors it could open for families. There were times I wished we could all get together in one place just to share life.

As I neared the end of 2014, I realized that it had been a year of pure growth and, even more unusual, a year without any significant roadblocks in the life of the cart. But as doors opened for the cart in new and expanded markets, I was more acutely aware of the companies that were still saying "no." I simply could not understand it. All of these stores that were closing the door had electric scooters and fun carts. What would it take for us to level the playing field?

I had been in sporadic conversations with large corporate retailers for years. But no matter which approach I tried, no matter which office I connected with or how many Caroline's Crusaders begged and pleaded with store managers, the answer from a few major retailers was always the same: No.

I heard time and time again that some special-needs families would change their shopping patterns during those years in favor of stores that offered a cart. Others used their Facebook or Instagram accounts to highlight the inequities in their shopping experiences. I never discouraged friends in the Caroline's Cart community from posting, because I kept hoping that the scales could be tipped by just one more heartfelt appeal.

As I kept tabs on the moms and dads who had signed on to the Caroline's Cart campaign, I realized that their passion for the cart could be a powerful public-relations tool. In January of 2015, I asked our Facebook followers to respond to the question, "Why should retailers provide Caroline's Cart?" I promised to use the responses in our appeals to stores throughout that year, and the responses were more heartfelt and convincing than anything a seasoned public relations firm could have crafted.

> My son has sensory issues. Because of Caroline's Carts, we can take him grocery shopping without meltdowns. He feels safe and is comfortable in the seat. If it is a choice between a store with lower prices or a store with a Caroline's Cart available, I will choose the store with a Caroline's Cart every time.
>
> —*Christina*

> I'm much more likely to shop somewhere where I don't have to lift my nine-year-old son into the basket. And seeing Caroline's Cart in a store shows me that they care about their customers with disabilities.
>
> —*Bonnie*

And this response painted a detailed picture of the reality of day-to-day life with a child who is unable to care for herself:

> When you have a child with special needs everything becomes so hard. There are days when I need to get errands done and visions of the time I took my daughter, who was six at the time, to change her diaper in a restaurant bathroom flood my memories. There was no changing table that could hold her, and I started to cry out of sheer frustration as I realized I would have to change her on the extremely soiled floor.
>
> The countless times I have to drag my crying, heartbroken child from the park because they don't have the swings that hold her properly. The time that I had to pull my daughter's wheelchair up a very long set of steps as there weren't any ramps. And particularly, the time I started bawling out of panic because I couldn't get my daughter, who had outgrown the front basket on shopping carts, out

of her seat and it required two full strangers to help me in a rainy parking lot just to get her out and into the car.

Caroline's Cart is more than a shopping cart. It is one less thing that tears away our strength to lead a normal day. The ability to get groceries, a simple thing, a necessity of life, is something that has drastically changed my strength as a parent of a child with special needs. I am a better parent because of it. There is more of me to go around mentally and emotionally. I cannot thank you enough for fighting your fight to get it to every parent or caregiver who needs it. You change lives and journeys in more ways than you know. ALL STORES IN 2015!!!!

I believe with all of my heart that if the executives in the retail food industry could read my Facebook wall, or if they walked in the shoes of any special-needs parent, we would soon see Caroline's Carts lined up at the entrance of every store in the nation. And there are countless other moms, including me, who have walked the same frustrating path and are just waiting for someone to throw them any kind of lifeline. It was incredibly gratifying to me that Caroline's Cart had become one of those lifelines to thousands of families, but it was aggravating in equal measure when I heard the daily complaints from parents who couldn't get their local stores to budge.

One big fish we had been working to catch for years was Target, a scenario that was complicated by the fact that the Target corporation had no pre-existing business relationship with Technibilt. Behind the scenes, the Technibilt sales team was negotiating with them about producing Caroline's Carts for them in their unique shade of red, which was darker than Technibilt's standard red. In early 2015 Target gave approval for managers to order the cart.

I was beside myself. Did Target just approve Caroline's Cart? *The* Target? The one with the red bull's-eye? I had been e-mailing Target since 2011, and it was hard to believe we had finally broken through.

I can't explain how much it meant to see the pictures of Target shoppers using Caroline's Cart. It represented such a huge leap in the story of the cart, and it gave all of us hope that the cart's presence could keep multiplying. There were certainly plenty of challenges ahead for me—both as a mom and an entrepreneur—but every month of 2015 brought a new cause for celebration.

Attempt something so impossible
that unless God is in it,
it is doomed to failure.

John Edmund Haggai

18

The Summer of (No) Fundo

IT HAD BEEN SIX YEARS since I had made those first phone calls and drove with trepidation to the meeting with Dr. Soni at UAB. When I decided to create the cart, my children were four, eight, and eleven. As we celebrated milestones like Target welcoming its first carts in the winter of 2015, they were ten, fourteen, and seventeen! My children had literally grown up with the cart, and I know at times we all felt like it was the fourth Long child.

I couldn't possibly count the times when my kids would get into the van in the carpool line and I would hold a finger to my lips, indicating that I was on a phone call for the cart and they needed to ride quietly. Or the nights when I was gone, on a trip to California or Ohio or North Carolina, and they had to improvise for dinner with good old dad, usually 1-800-Dominos. Caroline's Cart might have been my baby, but everyone in our family made sacrifices along the rocky road to its eventual success. And above all, my family's upbeat attitude towards the cart was only possible because of David's constant faithfulness and patience, even when I was the very opposite of steady and calm.

As the oldest, Mary Grace remembers the most about the good, the bad, and the ugly we Longs endured for the sake of the cart. For most of those years, she embraced the product and its mission, serving as one of my chief assistants and cheerleaders. As a participant in the Miss Alabama Outstanding Teen pageant in 2014 and 2015, she even chose Caroline's Cart as her platform. In the pageant world, a platform is the cause a contestant wants to use her title to raise awareness for or promote. She told the judges,

> My mom once said, I didn't choose my platform, my platform chose me, and that's really true because it's a lifestyle. It isn't something I just decided to pick up one day, it's something I've been living for the majority of my life.
>
> Everywhere I've gone, every time I talk about the cart, people are in awe. The reaction is always the same. First mesmerized and intrigued, then, "Why has no one thought of this before?" then, "I'm going to go look this up on Facebook."

But Mary Grace does recall, one day in middle school, feeling resentful toward the cart that seemed to be stealing all of my energy and focus.

I remember distinctly one day I was in the seventh grade. My mom picked me up in the carpool line, and I got in the car and she was on the phone with another lawyer, or another manufacturer or something, and it had been several days that this pattern had occurred, when I would get in the car and she'd be on the phone, and I'd get home and she would still be on the phone and I would go into my room and she would still be on the phone.

I remember thinking, "Ah, I've lost my mom. She is just so caught up in this cart. She is a stay-at-home mom, and all of a sudden she cares more about the cart than having a conversation with me on the way home from school."

That was my little thirteen-year-old mind that didn't really understand all the work and effort that had to go into something like that. But those days were gone really quickly, because I realized that was just part of it, and my mom is still my mom. As I look back now, I'm proud of the sacrifices we all had to make. It just took a while for me to get used to the idea that she was a working stay-at-home mom.

Matthew barely remembers a time when the cart wasn't part of our family landscape, and as a twelve-year-old he said that he liked the cool opportunities the cart provided—trips to New York City and Washington, D.C., his teacher's amazement when he told her I was on a trip to Germany. He also embraced his role in the cart's developmental years, when he would accompany me on those vital R & D trips to local grocery stores and leave with Skittles and a Sprite.

I knew that the kids and David were occasionally frustrated with the amount of time the cart consumed, and so was I. I didn't like the feeling that I had to give less of myself to them either. In this juggling act I was performing—essentially trying to be an attentive, involved stay-at-home mom who was also the founder of a demanding startup business venture—some of the balls inevitably hit the ground. But I prayed that this was just a season, and that this season too would pass.

All of us drew encouragement from the steady stream of good news people were sharing on social media. That's what kept me going, the reminder that so many were counting on me to finish what I had started. Early in the spring of 2015, Cub Foods in Minnesota became the latest chain to purchase carts for every one of its locations. A Cub store in the Twin Cities area had introduced the cart the previous year and it was so well-received that executives ordered one for each of their seventy-six stores less than a year later.

A Twin Cities Crusader named Lisa Jameson was instrumental in bringing the cart to Cub Foods. Her daughter Carly has Angelman Syndrome, and she was tireless both in her lobbying efforts at her local stores and in her encouragement of me as I labored across the country. I have never met her in person, but she even prayed with me over the phone one time when we talked; I will never forget that prayer and the boost of courage it gave me.

In April we heard good news about carts in stores in Australia, and more locations in Canada. That summer an Elks Club chapter in Canada took on the cart as a service project, raising money to place carts in several stores. The Elks Club has continued to be a vital advocate throughout Canada, helping bring carts to stores that might not otherwise be able to provide one. And that June, a Caroline's Crusader named Jenny Thomas posted the most popular photo that has ever been featured on any Caroline's Cart social media platform. The photo featured Thomas's ninety-one-year-old mother riding in the cart, and in the post Jenny explained how much more pleasant shopping was at her local Harris Teeter thanks to the cart. We hadn't even publicized the value of Caroline's Cart to seniors and their caregivers, but that single post and photo collected a mind-blowing twenty-five million views! Here's what she said:

> I asked my local Harris Teeter grocery store in Virginia if they had a shopping cart that I could put my ninety-one-year-old mother in. She likes to go with me to get her groceries but can no longer walk all the aisles. The options left me are to leave her in the car with it running, or she has to stay at home.

> Neither were good options. Turns out they had a Caroline's Cart and it worked perfect! I feel like your company has created a resource that could be so wonderful for seniors.
>
> Looking at the options in the lobby for carts [there] are the regular ones, the mini versions for children and the motorized ones which are wonderful for those who still have the skill set for driving. Nothing for elderly who have limited physical abilities at advanced ages but who still live at home and like to get out. By including seniors, caregivers can give seniors an option to get out of their recliners and back into the stores.

Sales and public relations were both on such a positive upswing as the summer of 2015 approached that I considered starting a book about the Caroline's Cart story. Walmart was still saying "no" to us, citing the cart's lack of safety certification from the American Society for Testing and Materials (ASTM), but despite that omission I felt confident that any book about the cart would still have a happy ending, with or without the nation's largest retailer on board. As it turns out, it was a blessing I didn't dive into a book project just then as my attentions were soon diverted elsewhere.

Caroline has digestive issues that make it difficult for her to process solid food, and before I traveled to Germany in 2014 she had a feeding tube put into her stomach so that she could be fed high-nutrient liquids directly through the tube. This was an improvement, but she had extreme reflux and would end up spitting up most of the milk about thirty minutes after every feeding. To combat this, her doctors scheduled another surgery called a fundoplication to correct the reflux problem. The fundo, as it is called, was supposed to be a simple laparoscopy procedure followed by a one-night hospital stay.

Of course, if you've noticed the trend, things that are supposed to be smooth and simple often turn out quite differently for the Long family. As I worked on Caroline's Cart correspondence on my trusty laptop in the waiting room, oblivious to what was going on in the operating room, doctors tried and failed over and over again to start the procedure using the scope. They changed course and opened Caroline up with traditional incisions, and when they did they discovered that her spleen was actually fused to her stomach!

Suddenly what had begun as a routine fundo procedure was an emergency surgery to separate two vital organs. Caroline lost so much blood that she needed two transfusions on the operating table, and eventually, with much difficulty, they were able to do the fundo. The doctors told us it was the most complicated one they had ever performed. It was an incredible ordeal—I found out later that Caroline could have died during that surgery—but the trials of that summer were just getting started.

All told, Caroline was admitted to the hospital three different times that summer and we spent at least six weeks in a hospital room. That summer was the second time I had completely missed Matthew's birthday. He turned eleven in July, and I never even laid eyes on him on his special day.

As Caroline recovered from major surgery, she battled several infections and recovered slowly. We were out getting food one night shortly after she was released and I got a hysterical phone call from Mary Grace, who was home with her sister. She was so upset I could hardly understand her. Caroline had suffered a major seizure and was turning blue. Mary Grace was understandably terrified. She called an ambulance and I rushed home to accompany Caroline yet again to the hospital, where she recovered from that emergency but contracted yet another infection.

Through that incredibly tumultuous season, I was doing my best to keep up with the steady demands of a cart that seemed to increase its global footprint every day. It was exciting—and a nice reprieve from endless days looking at hospital walls—to hear about another Target, another Costco, a store in New Zealand, a regional chain that ordered carts for every store. I was certainly never bored, because the Caroline's Cart activity online just kept multiplying. But on my personal Facebook page, I was petitioning my friends to pray for the very sick young lady for whom the cart was named. I felt God's faithfulness as I drew strength from their support.

My post from July 31 read,

> Third time's a charm? Had to bring Caroline back to the ER yesterday at 5 p.m. Started having lots of seizures. They admitted her to special care last night. We just came home this past Monday, still not near well, but hoping it was just the UTI and she would continue to heal at home. Well, no such luck. This all goes back to the July 6 surgery (which was supposed to be laparoscopic!). Since July 6, anything that could have gone wrong has gone wrong.

Slowly, after we were released from that hospital stay, Caroline recovered and gained her strength, and by the fall I had my girl back. In November, she was back to one hundred percent for a family trip to Disney World, believe it or not. It was while we were there that I got the exciting news that we had received our first order from Norway!

Fall was such a relief after the travails of summer, and even more so because of the national spotlight that seemed to be fixed on Caroline's Cart, with a splashy new feature every few weeks.

October brought a series of heartwarming articles, culminating in a story on *People* magazine's website about little Beatrice from Colorado Springs, who has cerebral palsy. Beatrice's mom Melody struggled to find a comfortable shopping option for her daughter, so she spoke to the manager of her local grocery store, King Sooper's, and soon he had ordered a Caroline's Cart for the location.

Adding to the appeal of the story was the fact that store employees had decorated the cart with colorful bows and a sign that read "Beatrice's Cart."

The cart was growing at a pace I had hardly dared to hope for back when I was still a renegade mom from Alabaster, Alabama, on a desperate hunt for a manufacturer. So many hurdles had already been cleared along the way, but I was determined (or stubborn) enough to aim for still more.

Commit your work to the Lord,
and your plans will be established.

Proverbs 16:3

19

Big Fish

NEAR THE END OF 2015, our positive buzz not only continued but the stories started to feature that store with the red bull's-eye. In November the online edition of ABC's *Good Morning America* jumped in, focusing on the Standiford family of Dardenne Prairie, Missouri, who had been liberated when they found a Caroline's Cart in a local Target store. When father Adam Standiford, whose daughter Savannah has a chromosomal disorder that has left her unable to walk, celebrated with a post on Facebook, it was shared over ten thousand times.

This dad was simply amazing in advancing our cause. His wife just happened to see a Caroline's Cart in Target and snapped a picture. Adam then posted a thank you message on the store's national Facebook page.

> Dear Target, I can't express enough how happy my wife was to see this at our local Target today.
>
> We have a six-year-old handicapped girl who either doesn't fit in carts anymore or gets weird looks as

> to why she's sitting in the basket and can't walk like a normal child. This simple cart literally will change how we can shop, not having to worry as to how we are going to get her into a store. Every retailer in the country should follow suit!

That simple act of advocacy for the cart gained so much mileage that soon ABC and others heard about Standiford and gave the cart even more platforms.

A feature in *Parents* magazine, also in November, drew readers in with the headline, YOU HAVE TO SEE THE TARGET SHOPPING CART THAT CHANGED A FAMILY'S LIFE, and *Good Housekeeping* printed a story that same month. I could have paid a public relations firm thousands of dollars a week and it couldn't possibly have generated this much good publicity in so many locations, with such a variety of uplifting stories about these beautiful children and their grateful parents who just want a typical shopping experience.

We couldn't deny that the entrance of Target into the Caroline's Cart world had amplified the media attention, and that reality made us even more hopeful that 2016 would bring more inroads into more major national chains.

Much to my amazement, the increased exposure even meant that I was recognized in public from time to time, a fact that was hilariously confirmed in an episode at the Birmingham Galleria Mall. As Matthew and I walked through a mob of people in the food court, a man came running after us.

"Are you the shopping cart lady?" he yelled at the top of his voice.

I had a nice chat with the man, a Georgia teacher who recognized me from videos about the cart, while Matthew stood by looking like he hoped the floor would swallow him up.

When Target customers continued to ask for Caroline's Cart, the company initiated talks with Technibilt about a national rollout. Earlier in 2015, when Target had put Caroline's Cart in twenty-four of its stores, customers like Standiford went crazy on social media. The response was so encouraging that in February 2016, Target announced that *all* its stores would soon have at least one cart.

It seems to me that Target, more than any other store, inspires a particular passion in moms. This groundbreaking announcement was one of our chief milestones in the odyssey of the cart—picking up the first prototype, the shipment of the first twelve carts from the initial manufacturer on Caroline's birthday, the agreement with Technibilt, and now, the comprehensive rollout with one of the nation's most respected and widespread retail chains. It's still hard for me to believe.

The decision first became public when Target issued a news release on February 4, detailing the history of the cart and the overwhelmingly positive response to the sampling of carts that had been tried in Target stores throughout the previous year. In my mind, trumpet fanfares were sounding when I read these remarks from Juan Galarraga, Target's senior vice president for store operations:

> Caroline's Cart can be a game-changer for families, and we're excited to offer this for our guests across the country. Target is always looking for new ways to make guests feel welcome in our stores and give them a more comfortable shopping experience.

Suddenly the Caroline's Crusaders who had been laboring and begging for years for the cart to gain a foothold in their towns had a lifeboat. Even if their local grocery store kept refusing or evading their entreaties, these faithful families were now guaranteed the opportunity to shop with a Caroline's Cart if they were near one of Target's eighteen hundred stores. The special-needs community responded with pure joy, and Target's announcement did more than anything previously to rally big-time media outlets around the cart.

In February the cart was featured on NBC's *Today Show*, which to me has always been the gold standard of morning television.

The best part about the *Today Show* story? I had no idea it was happening, and when I found out I was at the optometrist—with my eyes fully dilated!

My friend Amber sent me the following text:

> Drew, Caroline's Cart was just featured on *The Today Show*!

I could barely read the text with my eyes in that condition.

Frantically, I asked the eye doctor, "Hey, look at this, does that say 'The Today Show'?"

He confirmed that my cart had indeed hit the big time, and I promptly informed him that I had to get out of there immediately. I put on two pair of those dark plastic glasses, took a minute to text David and some people at Technibilt, and took off in search of a video clip.

The "News with Natalie" segment featured a short story about the cart, complete with footage of me pushing Caroline in one of our promotional videos!

The sweetest memory from the *Today Show* coverage was Mary Grace's reaction on Facebook when she heard about it during one of her high school classes:

> I was sitting in fifth period study hall today when my teacher mentioned, "How about your mom being on *The Today Show* this morning? Pretty cool, huh?"
>
> I immediately froze and I'm pretty sure my heart stopped for a couple of seconds. Then I went to Mrs. Mitchell's room, a loving teacher, wonderful family friend, and faithful prayer warrior for the cart, to watch the *Today Show* footage. And sure enough, there was Natalie Morales talking about my mom. My family and I have been fervently praying for God to open the door to allow Caroline's Cart to be on the national news networks. This is what we have been waiting for.

> Excited, happy, proud, grateful, and relieved are the emotions flooding my house right now, but of all those emotions, the way I feel most is proud—proud of my mom. While we have always said that the cart is a family project, there are no doubts in my mind that my mom has done the majority of it. My mom has been tirelessly working on the cart for more than eight years.
>
> Was it hard? Absolutely. Was it frustrating? Yes. But it was God's plan for her life, and she clearly understood that, so she did not lose heart and refused to quit. Galatians 6:9 says, "And let us not grow weary of doing good, for in due season we will reap, if we do not give up." She did not give up, and now she is reaping the many benefits that she more than deserves. This is the season of fruition.

Oh, how my heart melted when I read this! All the accolades in the world can't compare to words like these from your child, who has been on this journey with you and knows the sacrifices it required.

Also in February, a *Fortune* magazine story highlighted the fact that Target was the largest retailer in the nation to supply carts to all of its stores. *The Huffington Post* published an article in early May centered on a St. George, Utah, mom named Rebecca, who wrote an open letter to Target on Facebook which read, in part,

> This is a game changer for families like mine. It means I can shop without having to push a cart and pull a wheelchair. It means my little girl can participate in one more aspect of life. We are beyond excited about it.

Because of the Target news, CNN got hold of the story and sent a film crew to my house. They ran the resulting piece on their CNN Airport network. It was fun to hear from friends around the country who saw the story while waiting for their flights!

These media outlets learned about the cart in a variety of ways, but sometimes a special-needs parent worked at the company and gave us the inside track. That's what happened with iHeart Radio, which took notice because an associate producer and special-needs mom named Darlene Rodrigo loved the cart and thought it should be featured on one of iHeart's shows. Soon I was on the phone with one of their famous Los Angeles-based DJs, Ellen K, who interviewed me for the "Feelgood Friday" segment of her show. (*Hmmm . . . I wonder if Ellen D listens to Ellen K? She loves a good human interest story. I'm keeping my phone close at hand, just in case.*)

iHeart Radio loved the story so much that they also interviewed me for a longer segment on one of their Sunday morning shows. Darlene, an amazing West Coast advocate for the cart, also lobbied CBS Los Angeles to do a big story when Target unveiled the cart nationwide.

Put simply, Target doesn't decide to do anything in every one of its stores without making some significant national waves. And our ambitious 2016 fishing trip wasn't finished yet. With Target getting all kinds of good PR for its Caroline's Cart rollout, other chains took notice. One company that we started having hopeful conversations with was a certain behemoth from Arkansas.

Technibilt's Walmart backstory involved the megastore's stringent requirements for safety standards. Essentially, the executives in Arkansas were asking Alan Deal at Technibilt to write a new set of ASTM standards for a special-needs cart, since such a standard didn't exist before we developed Caroline's Cart. That process doesn't happen quickly, but Walmart agreed to start ordering carts on a case-by-case basis while the ASTM benchmarks were being finalized.

And then, sure enough, there it is, a red letter day on the Technibilt sales spreadsheet—February 29, 2016. Just two weeks after a flood of Target orders consumed the Technibilt production line, Alice Little received ... drumroll, please ... our first two U.S. Walmart orders, for stores in Oklahoma City, Oklahoma, and American Fork, Utah! We had celebrated big-time a year earlier when a few Canadian Walmart stores had ordered the cart, but it had taken a while for U.S. Walmarts to follow suit. It wasn't a nationwide rollout, but Walmart managers now had permission to order when customers requested. And because I knew the Caroline's Cart community, I knew that these early initial orders were about to go from a snowball into an avalanche.

In March and April we were sticking virtual pins representing Walmart locations all over the map—Arkansas, Illinois, Texas, Missouri, Washington, D.C., and lots of stores in my own home state. That spring, at long last, Caroline and I went on a landmark shopping trip in our own hometown Alabaster, Alabama, Walmart. Of course, we celebrated by posting a video on the Caroline's Cart Facebook page.

That excursion with Caroline was a poignant reminder of God's faithfulness, because in the dry years of the cart, when I felt like every effort drove me into another brick wall, I used to drop the kids off at school, drive to Walmart, sit in my car in the parking lot, and pray. I remember just sitting there praying, telling the Lord that I was giving Him authority over the journey of the cart and every decision I made along the way. I prayed that He would bless my efforts and that He would open doors for it. I even prayed specifically that Walmarts around the world would carry it. So when I was able to push my daughter through the aisles of that same Walmart in a Caroline's Cart, it was like a mountain had moved before my very eyes.

Walmart carts were being unveiled and trumpeted left and right through the first half of 2016, and every day I answered questions from shoppers still hoping to add their Walmart to the growing list. Soon after the Target rollout, we were thrilled to see movement from other sectors of the industry, with Home Depot collaborating with Technibilt to create carts in their trademark orange, and new carts popping up in Sam's Club, Costco, Pier 1, and even one Party City location.

I can't even express to you what an exciting season this was for my family, my partners at Technibilt, and every person who had given time and energy to the cart over those difficult years in the desert. Target and Walmart, in just a few short months? As I had always hoped and prayed, this thing had become far bigger than me, and it seemed that we were truly watching the evolution of a new standard in the retail industry.

In a massive leap from the early social media days when I would celebrate a hundred likes on a post, an online human-interest outlet called Upworthy profiled Caroline's Cart in early July, and we were blown away by the number of people who were reached. Less than two months after the site first told our story, the post had collected *millions* of views. We have been intentional about giving God the glory through the peaks and the valleys, and numbers like that are humbling and thrilling because I know they will lead to more families being helped and, ultimately, more people learning about the Lord's hand in bringing this cart to reality.

Buoyed by these successes, that spring David and I decided the time was right to tell our story in this book, and I also started accepting speaking engagements so that others could be encouraged by the journey that could have so easily ended in failure. It was far from an easy road, and I'm still traveling down it, but God had a purpose for every pitfall as He grew my faith and created a platform for me to be a cheerleader for others who are beset by difficulties on their way to pursuing a dream.

The last time I had visited the Technibilt plant had been for the winter sales meeting, when those in attendance were moved to tears by the video of smiling children using the cart across the U.S. and the globe. We had plenty of new things to celebrate in the few short months since that trip, and in the hottest part of July I packed up for another drive to North Carolina, where the group of people who spend their days occupied by the manufacture, marketing, and sale of Caroline's Cart had started to feel more like family than colleagues.

Life's most persistent
and urgent question is:
"What are you doing for others?"

Martin Luther King, Jr.

20

Pressing On

NO TRIP WAS EVER SIMPLE in my world, so in July 2016 as I prepared to be away from home for a couple of days for the visit to Technibilt I still had a dizzying number of things on my to-do list so that life would run smoothly in my absence. Adding to the normal tasks related to caring for Caroline, driving Matthew to various places, and keeping tabs on my mom (who was in the midst of chemotherapy treatments), was our upcoming big Long family event. Mary Grace was packing for her move to Auburn University in early August, where she would move into the dorm as a freshman.

This is a milestone I was certainly not prepared for. Mary Grace is my pal, and the rest of us were not ready to be a household of four. Who would watch the Miss America pageant and *Dancing With The Stars* with me? On top of that, she has long been my social media guru and one of my best editors; I am accustomed to having her read everything before I post it online.

After fifteen years as the parents of a daughter with special needs, we had much of Caroline's care on auto pilot—setting up her cans of Ensure for the daily feedings through her feeding tube, feeding her by mouth once a day to give her more variety of taste and texture, changing her diapers, moving her from the wheelchair to the therapeutic chair or her bed. (We have to move her about every two hours during the day to ward off bedsores and pressure sores.) But without warning, at times a seizure, an illness, or some other issue would throw our well-scripted routine into chaos. One such hiccup came our way in 2016 over Memorial Day weekend.

David and Mary Grace had gone to Auburn to register Mary Grace for fall classes, but holding down the fort with the other two kids had become routine for me. We would order takeout, watch movies—no big deal. That is, until I threw my back out, making it impossible for me to pick up my eighty-five-pound daughter to move her in or out of the wheelchair. Matthew helped me as much as he could but he was a twelve-year-old boy, not a grown man, so we improvised some things. We put Caroline on a sheet and dragged her from room to room when we had to, and we made a bed on the floor so she could sleep there until either my back improved or David returned. That's life, and I know many other parents can relate, but it wasn't the laid back weekend I had envisioned.

In the dim days after Caroline's diagnosis, we had resolved that we would never seek pity or see ourselves—or Caroline—as victims. I hope we've done a good job at maintaining that attitude over the years, but in doing so I know that people around us forget about challenges like the Memorial Day weekend incident. We don't talk about it much, so they aren't aware that we have to feed Caroline with a tube several times a day no matter where we are, and we know that tube feeding in public makes some people uncomfortable so we take pains to cover up with a big towel.

They don't know that going out on our pontoon boat takes extra effort since the wheelchair doesn't roll on the boat, or that a wheelchair doesn't roll on the beach, unless the hotel has a special beach wheelchair, so a vacation to the coast is far from relaxing for Caroline or her parents. They don't know that when we change her diaper in public, we are forced to lay her down on dirty bathroom floors. They don't know that Caroline could have a seizure at any moment without warning, drastically altering our plans for that day.

We don't whine or complain about those kinds of things; we love our daughter and we are glad to do whatever we need to do to keep her safe and healthy. But just as the Caroline's Cart campaign allowed me and others to shine a light on the struggles of grocery shopping with kids like Caroline, we have the opportunity to remind the world of the challenges so many families have to work through each day.

So when I traveled, as I did fairly often on cart business, I left David with plentiful instructions and made sure friends and neighbors were on call to help him if something unusual should occur. The drive up to North Carolina on that steamy July day for the Technibilt meeting gave me several hours to reflect and pray—for Mary Grace in her new chapter, for the growth of the cart, for everyone in my family to keep God and His plan for them first.

I arrived late in the afternoon, had dinner with my dear friend Alice Little, and checked into a hotel to sleep before reporting to Technibilt early the next morning.

In many ways, it was a typical Technibilt visit—I caught up with Alice, Alan Deal, Gary Soden, and David Orfinik, who had been my advocates at that company since I first showed up there, terrified, for a meeting with Alan in 2010. I enjoyed the chance to talk with Klaus-Dieter Wurm, the new Technibilt CEO. I got sales updates, discussed upcoming trade shows and other special events, and, as part of my research for this book, looked at some photos from the past three years.

The high-water mark of the day for me was the tour of the plant floor, which is always fascinating because of the processes and materials that go into creating hundreds of grocery carts each day. Not just Caroline's Carts, of course, but all types of carts for all types of stores. I had put on earplugs and walked through the plant before, but for the first time that day Alice and I made a video for the Caroline's Cart Facebook page to give our cart family an inside look at the product and encourage them to keep plugging along if the cart had not yet made it to their store.

The video showed Alex Burgess, one of the technicians assigned to Caroline's Cart, doing some of the manual assembly. And as I spoke about the latest progress on the cart, the camera panned down several long, colorful rows of Caroline's Carts—all just waiting for a store to order them so that they could be shipped out.

In that long line were blue Kroger carts, red Target carts, gray Publix carts, and another group of lighter green carts I was seeing for the first time, hot off the production line and ready to ship to Walmart Neighborhood Markets. That line of carts was one of the most encouraging things I had seen in a while, but it didn't represent the finish line of this quest that had defined my past eight years.

I had been there before, but this trip was different; I was absolutely overcome with gratitude and humility. I had been a witness to the fulfillment of God's promise, and it was as if He was saying, "I did everything I told you I would do."

We are certainly gaining ground every day, and I believe that our small victories are leading to a world in which Caroline's Cart truly is the new standard—an essential piece of equipment for every store. The momentum is on our side, and with our game-changing cart we will make it happen. But I find myself getting frustrated with the obstacles that still stand in our way.

Some of the most encouraging stories posted on our social media pages were at the same time the most maddening. I can't possibly count the number of times I have read an e-mail or a post with a message like this:

> I have been begging my store manager for more than two years, stopping every time I come into the

store to ask him to order a Caroline's Cart. He told me a month ago that the store had finally ordered one, and yesterday I cried tears of joy when my son and I were able to shop in it for the first time!

With every post like that, we move the ball a little further down the field, but those stories also make me wonder, "Why do people have to beg?" It makes me crazy. Call me a broken record if you want, but do they beg store managers for years asking their store to get an electric scooter? The cart is now readily available and has passed all safety requirements, and its surging popularity has proved that the need is real. The fact that families are still begging for months or years on end—and then thanking stores profusely when they finally come through—just doesn't seem right.

Often physical progress is easier to achieve than a shift in attitudes, and we are trying to advocate for a mindset of equal access that would truly make Caroline's Cart the new standard for stores everywhere. We are trying to change the retail culture. When Alice gets phone calls from Girl Scout troops or Kiwanis clubs wanting to raise money to buy and donate a cart, she thanks them for their interest and tells them that such fundraising isn't necessary. They just need to print some "Dear Store Manager" letters and brochures and canvass their local grocery stores.

The Caroline's Cart Facebook, Twitter, and Instagram accounts remain very busy, because at least once a day an exultant parent posts a picture of a child or adult shopping in a cart for the first time. Those posts never cease to inspire me, and even though we no longer have to raid our savings accounts to further the cart, I will always consider the stories of cart successes the best type of paycheck I can receive.

The ultimate victory isn't in hand yet, but we believe that this game will end in a resounding victory if the army of Caroline's Crusaders keeps pressing on. With Technibilt in my corner and the progress the cart is making daily, we can truly call Caroline's Cart a game changer in the world of special-needs accommodation and a new standard in the retail industry. I have no intention of slowing down in my quest to see the cart in every store.

That long row of colorful carts at Technibilt that afternoon inspired gratitude in me—it was a beautiful picture of God's faithfulness through what once seemed to be miles of desolate wilderness. He asked us to stay the course, through hundreds of thousands of dollars spent with no promise of return, through countless closed doors from people in the industry who were vital to our success, through surgeries and layoffs and crazy weeks when my husband and children needed me to keep things going at home but Caroline's Cart needed me to be a full-time CEO as well.

There is much ahead for us—the continued infiltration of Caroline's Cart into stores, media coverage, speaking engagements, communication with the moms and dads who need a cheerleader. We are excited to announce the formation of our non-profit, Caroline's Cause, that will give us a platform to further raise awareness about needs and solutions in the special-needs community. One way or another, the cart will be a central part of my family's life and mine forever, and we wouldn't have it any other way.

I pray that whenever any of us is tempted to lay down the sword in a battle the Lord has given us to fight, we will plant our feet and persevere, confident that He is our source of strength. Above all, we want God to get the glory for the unlikely story of a mom who identified a need, birthed a crazy dream to meet that need, and traveled a tumultuous road to see that dream become a reality.

I can't think of a better way to put a final punctuation mark on the story of this remarkable adventure than with Galatians 6:9, the verse Mary Grace posted on Facebook the day Caroline's Cart was featured on *The Today Show*: "Let us not grow weary of doing good, for in due season we will reap, if we do not give up."

I'm not giving up—don't you give up, either!

When I left [Yale], I didn't have much in the way of a life plan. I knew some people who thought they did. But it turned out that we were all in for ups and downs, most of them unexpected. Life takes its own turns, makes its own demands, writes its own story. And along the way, we start to realize we are not the author.

George W. Bush

Afterword

Final thoughts

I BELIEVE THAT IN THE life of every great idea or invention, there comes a time when those responsible must decide to either move forward or simply chalk up their idea as just that ... a good idea, but a good idea whose time is not now. The scariest time in all of this journey was not right at the beginning when the idea was fresh and new. That was actually an exciting time when there was not much else to do except talk. Talk is easy. Talk is cheap. And talk is often fun. But talk rarely gets things done! Once you've bored your spouse and your family and your close friends to the point of exasperation, there comes a time for that scariest decision of all ... Are we *really* going to do this?

For me and David, the decision to move forward was that time when the fear of not knowing "what might have been" outweighed the fear of committing ourselves financially. In other words, *Could we live with not knowing if the cart would make it, or was finding out the answer to that question worth the price of admission and worth the possibility of complete failure?*

That's what I would tell any budding entrepreneur. "Would you be okay not knowing?" If the answer to that question is "yes," or even a "maybe," I would instruct them to STOP NOW!

To take a leap of faith like we had to do for the cart, the option of not knowing can't be an option! The motivation and unwavering commitment to the idea has to transcend any potential financial return. For us, that was made easier by viewing Caroline's Cart as a legacy for our daughter and by praying for and receiving clear guidance and wisdom along the way.

But even still, there's a necessary ingredient that must exist even before the financial decisions begin. That's boldness! Being bold ... specifically, being bold in your faith ... is a slippery slope. Too much and your boldness can turn into pride or arrogance. Nothing clouds sound decision-making more than pride. Too little and you'll never convince yourself or anyone else that your idea has merit. The motivation will wane and you simply won't be equipped to weather the storms that will invariably come your way. Finding that balance is not often easy (I struggled with it, too!) but is critical for success.

I wholeheartedly believe that everyone has a purpose and possesses the potential to be a "game changer." Your purpose might not be a new invention, but if it is from God it will be *your* "game changer."

What's more, I honestly believe that God will reveal to each of us what that purpose is ... if we're faithful in our walk with Him and willing to respond with obedience.

Over these past years my family has grown and changed and been challenged and tested through many trials, but we are forever committed to Caroline's Cart. The Crusaders who have messaged me, posted pictures of your precious children using the cart, prayed for me, and talked incessantly to store managers, have been the lifeblood of this battle, and I feel like I know you all. Thank you from the bottom of my heart. All of you, mostly people I've never met, were my manna from heaven. Time after time, you helped me stay the course when quitting seemed like the smart thing to do.

I hope my story has encouraged you to persevere through whatever you are facing. The most vital lesson I have learned is that God's way and timing are not the same as mine, and that just because God gives us a mission doesn't mean it will be easy to see that cause become a reality. You will face adversity and the worst of storms—that I can promise! Your foundation must be strong and steadfast.

I've learned to see the good within the bad and to realize that God's path for my life is the only one I want to walk, even when that path is incredibly rocky.

We are proud that our daughter Caroline has an incredible legacy—one that has now helped so many families and helped to transform an industry. We will continue to support any cause that helps create equal access for special needs families and pray for further opportunities to share this amazing story of God's power to use a shopping cart (of all things!) for His glory.

The book is over but our story, and this journey, will continue. As this book about to go to press Caroline's Cart was one of twenty-five honorees on the "List of People Shaping Retail's Future 2017," an award that included an invitation to a gala sponsored by the National Retail Federation Foundation. This award is more than an honor, it affirms that Caroline's Cart has broken barriers, and that our voice has been heard. Receiving national recognition solidifies the belief that together, we can all make a difference. New doors seem to open every week, and each new pathway intensifies our hope that the cart will one day be found in every store, everywhere.

I believe it was Mark Twain who said, "You're never wrong to do the right thing," and this quote comes to mind when I think of the many people who helped to make Caroline's Cart a reality. I want to thank my amazing team who gave of their time and resources early on when I only had a dream and a drawing. Your efforts were not in vain; you all made a difference in the lives of every Caroline's Cart user.

To Rebel, who believed in this from day one, who believed in me, and whose fearless determination to see this through was unstoppable, thank you!

To my friends at Technibilt, Caroline's Cart is only where it is today because of you. Thank you for a quality product and your continued commitment to promoting accessibility and equal access in *all* retail stores.

And of course I have to thank Bethany Bradsher who did such an amazing job helping me put my story down on paper. You are so talented and were truly a joy to work with.

To my children and husband David—words are simply inadequate to express my feelings of intense gratitude. Your tireless sacrifice and support during this journey have been simply amazing. I love you.

And lastly, to you, the readers of this book—I wish you great joy and success as you chase your dreams. I'll be your biggest fan and cheerleader. I hope every time you see or use a Caroline's Cart you will think of that mom from Alabaster, Alabama, who dared to dream big. Happy shopping, sweet tea, and M&M's!

Your forever shopping cart lady,
—DREW ANN LONG

"Now to Him who is able to do infinitely more than all we ask or imagine, according to His power that is at work within us, to Him be the glory."
Ephesians 3:20–21 (BSB)

For more information about booking Drew Ann Long for a speaking engagement, email bookings@carolinescart.com.

Follow Caroline's Cart and Drew Ann Long on Facebook, Twitter, Instagram, and YouTube. Just search for carolinescart!

Acknowledgments

AL.com
The Allen Family
Brad Anderson
Bradley Arant Boult Cummings LLP
Sarah Brewster
Gene Cary
Easter Seals
The Egbert Family
Nicole Fochtmann Photography
Michael Garry
John Marc Green
Deborah Herbert
iHeart Radio
The Innovation Depot
Dennis Leonard
Michael Marks
Randy McClanahan
Sean McDonald
Mike Murphy
Rebel Negley
John Ondrasik
Brendon Pinola Photography
Darlene Rodrigo
Darlene Rotch
Shelby County Reporter
Supermarket News
Technibilt
University of Alabama at Birmingham (UAB)
V Richards
The Wanzl Family
The Yenisehirli Family
Zoo Fuse

Indesign

Griffin Bryce, Director of Business Development
Jerry Gotway, President and Project Manager
Darrin Newbold, Senior Engineering Associate
Mehul Patel, Mechanical Engineer
Chris Shea, Senior Engineering Associate
Adam Whitesell, Mechanical Engineer

Colophon

Book designed and edited by Kit Sublett
Cover designed by Stephanie W. Dicken
Main body composed in Fournier MT Standard,
a font by Pierre Simon Fournier le jeune, and set at 11.5/15
Chapter titles and epigraphs composed in Futura